Books by Lavinia Russ

A YOUNG EXPLORER'S NEW YORK:
MAPS OF MANHATTAN

OVER THE HILLS AND FAR AWAY

FOREVER ENGLAND:
POETRY AND PROSE ABOUT ENGLAND AND THE ENGLISH

THE GIRL ON THE FLOOR WILL HELP YOU

A HIGH OLD TIME

A HIGH
OLD TIME

or
How to Enjoy Being a
Woman over Sixty

———— ❧❦❧ ————

LAVINIA RUSS

Saturday Review Press

NEW YORK

For "Everyone Sang" from *Collected Poems* by Siegfried Sassoon. Copyright 1920 by E. P. Dutton & Co., renewed in 1948 by Siegfried Sassoon. All rights reserved. Reprinted by permission of The Viking Press, Inc. and George Sassoon.

For "News Item" and extract from "Inventory" from *The Portable Dorothy Parker*. Copyright 1926, © renewed 1954 by Dorothy Parker. All rights reserved. Reprinted by permission of The Viking Press, Inc.

For extract from "An Old Woman of the Roads" from *Wild Earth and Other Poems* by Padraic Colum. All rights reserved. Reprinted by permission of Padraic Colum.

For "For Poets" from *The Song Turning Back into Itself* by Al Young. Copyright © 1971 by Al Young. Reprinted by permission of Holt, Rinehart and Winston, Inc.

Published simultaneously in Canada by
Doubleday Canada Ltd., Toronto.

Library of Congress Catalog Card Number: 70-154272

ISBN 0-8415-0148-3

Saturday Review Press
230 Park Avenue, New York, New York 10017

PRINTED IN THE UNITED STATES OF AMERICA
SECOND PRINTING
Design by Tere LoPrete

FOR—
*Two magnificent children,
two magnificent friends:
Margaret and Michael Geiger*

*And a grateful wave
to the unflappable Joellyn Ausanka*

Everyone suddenly burst out singing;
And I was filled with such delight
As prisoned birds must find in freedom
Winging wildly across the white
Orchards and dark green fields; on; on; and out of sight.

Everyone's voice was suddenly lifted,
And beauty came like the setting sun.
My heart was shaken with tears; and horror
Drifted away. . . . O, but everyone
Was a bird; and the song was wordless; the singing will
    never be done.

Everyone Sang BY *Siegfried Sassoon*

Arnold L. Lambert bought this book
at
Kitsap Regional Library
in
Bremerton, Wa
on
4-8-1996
for
$1/12¢

Contents

❧⸎❧

A HIGH OLD TIME

I

The Best Is Yet to Be, My Foot

I started writing this book when I was ten years old. I made the first note for it one day when my mother sent me over to my grandmother's house. "Go keep her company," Mother had said. "She gets lonely." I didn't mind going: Gammie was a pretty, pink-and-white old lady (old to me *then;* she was all of sixty-two), she always had gooey cookies for me, and as I brushed her fine white hair, she'd tell me stories about the old days when she was little. It was while I was brushing her hair that the first entry for this book popped up. Gammie hadn't dressed yet; for the first time, as she sat in her cotton nightgown by the window, I saw her upper arms, and they repulsed me. She wasn't fat, but there was a hanging ruffle of flesh on the underside of her arms, from her elbow up, that wavered as she rocked, and I thought, when *I* get to be an old lady, I'll never let anybody see *my* upper arms. And my Old Lady Book was born.

I've been an old-lady watcher ever since. Old ladies have fascinated me from the beginning: crotchety or benign, feisty or serene, imperious or comic, they all seemed to be characters, individualists in their own right. I loved them all. I listened and eavesdropped to what they said, listened and eavesdropped to what younger people said about them, which characteristics and habits they admired in old ladies, which ones sent them up the wall.

I was sure I'd never utter the infinitely sad cry of Dorothy Parker—"Promise me, promise me I won't get old," she would say when she was already there—because, unlike a lot of women, I *knew* I was going to be sixty someday, and knew, too, that the sixties would be a great proving ground to test the way I would be when I was seventy, and eighty, and all the way. After I turned forty and got embroiled in fashion and fashion shows, I started jotting down the things that women in their sixties and up did to enhance themselves. And the things they did that made them either grotesque or pathetic, two adjectives I would never invite when *I* hit the sixties.

Because, at fifty, I started to earn my living by writing, I had a hunch the notes might turn into a book someday. A question kept the hunch vague: how could I transform these notes into a book that was convincing when I had not yet sampled the decade myself? If it were written by a woman who hadn't reached her sixties, it would arouse the same doubts as a book entitled *How to Find a Million Dollars in Your Sleep*. For if the writer had found the million, he'd be too busy to write the book, too busy pacing the deck of his yacht, en route to the Riviera, to bother.

It wasn't until I hit my sixties that I added the word *enjoy* to my scenario for *How to Be a Woman over Sixty.* I added it because I have enjoyed my seven years in the sixties. I have enjoyed them because I have accepted the fact that I *am* an old lady, which has made me not only the founder and president, but the only member of the Revolutionary Order of Old Women Against Youth. (Initialed, it becomes ROOOWAY; said out loud, it has a pleasantly raffish sound.) For practically nobody dares admit to being an old lady. Not today, when if to be young is very heaven, to be old is very hell, and women fight grimly to deny it.

Not *me.* I think youth is heaven, though sadly enough we are not aware of it at the time, or aware we are in the process of writing our own play. "Your young self?" wrote Sybille Bedford. "Ah well, one does odd things. You see, when one is young one doesn't feel part of it yet, the human condition: one does things because they are not for good: everything is a rehearsal. To be repeated ad lib, to be put right when the curtain goes up in earnest. One day you know that the curtain was up all the time. That *was* the performance."

If I'd been around when Robert Browning first read his lines "Grow old along with me! The best is yet to be," I would have told him that he was out of his skull. Of course, he was probably trying to sell Elizabeth and himself on the glories of a middle-aged romance, as they were both a little on the sere side when they got married. But given the choice, what woman on earth would choose old age over youth?

((5))

But you don't *have* a choice. That's the truth of it. You may drift along for years, feeling safely insulated in a time bubble in which you forever stay a woman of about forty—certainly no longer a young woman, but just as certainly not an old one—until one day a casual crack from a friend, a look from a stranger breaks the bubble, and wham! you are sixty. And you know it.

My first hint came on a Fifth Avenue bus, when I got up to give my seat to a white-haired woman and saw, in her outraged face, the knowledge that I was older than she. But the full revelation came the day I was retired. After six weeks there would be no more pay checks. I said "Thank you" to the publisher of the magazine where I was an editor, put on my coat, got into a cab, wondered all the way to Fifty-second Street why I'd said "Thank you," bought the caftan I'd been dreaming about ever since I'd seen it in the *Times*, took another taxi home, put on the caftan, and sat down and figured out how much money I had. With $37.50 in the bank plus the severance pay the publisher had mentioned, I would have enough to continue as is for two months if I stayed out of cabs and leaned hard for breakfast and lunch on Metrecal cookies. Two months of the balance of my days. I was sixty-seven and I came from a long line of people who live forever.

I took off the caftan, put on a nightgown, and went to bed and immediately to sleep, as if I'd been hit over the head with a baseball bat.

I woke up in the gray-green light that comes before daylight. The panics had waked me: they had established their headquarters in my stomach. They always make for the stomach. I visualize them down there, part of a ghoulish experiment in the laboratory of Bela Lugosi; they leap back and forth from one steaming beaker to another, a hysterical parade of flashing electrons.

I sat up, lighted a cigarette, and said out loud that old standby of war movies: "Well, what do you know? This *is* it!" There was nobody around to argue the point. Peakie, my schnauzer, sighed at being displaced from her spot in the small of my back, circled a couple of times, and went back to sleep. I went on talking out loud: "That crack that what you fear most never happens is unadulterated hogwash! I've been squeaking for years, like the White Queen in *Alice* before she was pricked with her brooch, What will I do when I retire? Where will I live? What will I use for money? O.K. Now I've *been* retired. What *will* I do?"

Suddenly, as clearly as if she were really standing there, I saw my mother: a wild, zestful Irishwoman, often a pain in the neck to her family because she was always on stage, and always stage center, the star in a production that began the day she learned to talk and continued until the night she died. I thought, All right, Ma. I've got to find a new part for myself, have got to write, finance, costume, and direct a new production. It won't be a play about a dominating mother. All three of my children, thank God, have grown up to be too strong for me to dominate. I'll never be the superstar that you were, but I'm glad I had a ham for a mother. I'll be a ham, too. At first I thought I would snitch a title for my play from a couplet of Dorothy Parker's:

Three be the things I shall have till I die:
Laughter and hope and a sock in the eye.

But, better still, I decided to go straight to the point and call it *A High Old Time*, adding, in case anyone missed my point, *How to Enjoy Being a Woman over Sixty*.

Mother faded away. The panics stopped leaping from beaker to beaker. I pushed Peakie over and went peacefully back to sleep.

When I woke up the next morning I started the game I'm still playing—defining and redefining my role for the sixties. Before I made any choice, I wanted to look over women in the news—famous women in their sixties and up—compare their styles, decide which was the most suitable to my resources, and adapt it. A flock of names came to mind. The first to surface was Rose Kennedy. She had made a perfect landing on the planet of the over-sixties and has survived there with great style since, despite the tragedies in her life. But I don't possess the benefits of her faith, though I envy her for having it. Or her money. And I can't play golf.

Joan Crawford I discarded the moment I thought of her. It would take too much time as well as money to achieve her perfect, lacquered look. I wouldn't want it, anyway. She looks as if she'd melt away, like plastic, if left out in the heat of the noonday sun.

Bette Davis was tempting—a gutsy woman, she has accepted her age: the wrinkles, the pouches under the eyes, the whole rotten mess of getting old. She is her own woman, and always has been. I was a little too shaky right then to be that certain of myself.

I ran into the same trouble with Katharine Hepburn. She established a style long ago that I admire, but I look like hell in pants and don't like showers enough even to contemplate the eight she takes every day. Nor do I have the most remote chance of ever becoming, like her, a Legend in My Time.

There was Britain's Queen Mother, as comfortable as a ball of yarn. But I am no earl's daughter, and if I tried to carry off the fussy pastel dresses and the plume-ringed hats she wears, I'd burst out laughing at myself when I passed a mirror.

Then there were, for me, the impossible dreams, the women whose great talents or endowments were responsible for their indomitable spirits: Georgia O'Keefe, Rebecca West, Martha Graham, Gladys Cooper, Margaret Chase Smith. I'd love to pick Beatrice Lillie—the funniest woman in the world, too funny to try to imitate. Marlene Dietrich? I didn't have her beautiful legs or her skill in the kitchen. Marian Anderson with her warm and lyrical voice—but I can't carry a tune from here to the front door. Marianne Moore, crisp in her three-cornered hat—but no poet, I. Margaret Mead, too intellectual to bother how she looks. I'm too unintellectual *not* to bother. And the most impossible dream of all, Greta Garbo, endowed by her beautiful bones with a beauty the years can never diminish.

Mae West swiveled in and exited laughing. Jolie Gabor I threw out: she looks like a blurred edition of her daughters, who are beginning to look like blurred editions of themselves.

I didn't consider Helen Hayes; she's little, I'm big. And she's charming and I've always been afraid of charm— there's the danger inherent that it may turn arch while you're looking at it.

Arch or formidable—the women who have not only survived but conquered the hazards of age seem to be one or the other. And me? I decided to choose for my model the most formidable lady of all, Alice Roosevelt Longworth. I'm choosing her because she *is* a lady and therefore can defy fashion by wearing only what most becomes her (has worn the same style of wide-brimmed hat forever), can defy convention by saying what she thinks, and because she so obviously enjoys being an old lady, is proud to be a great lady who is old. I'm choosing her because she has accepted with grace her sixties—and on up. With grace—now *there* is the most becoming as well as the most flattering light for a woman of any age to bask in.

And the most relaxing. For once you have accepted the sixties, once you have made an honest inventory of your assets and debits, your figure, clothes, money, health, interests, hobbies, skills, you can start to create a new design for living, a sixty-year-old pattern that you will enjoy. It's true. I promise you, it's true.

And I'm the woman who can promise it because I am having a high old time in my sixties.

II

Boring from Within

The greatest weapon in our family arsenal was the phrase "You're being a bore"— an insult indigenous to the twenties and thirties when the writers who influenced conduct were men and women who preferred death to boredom. It was the time of the Algonquin Round Table, where the wit of Dorothy Parker bloomed, alongside that of George S. Kaufman and S. J. Perelman. And of *The New Yorker* when it was young, where James Thurber flourished, with E. B. White and Frank Sullivan, and that benign wit Robert Benchley, who did the impossible and was witty without wounding.

To entertain is a respectable virtue. It's not one that conventional moralists make much of, although it is astounding how many of Thomas Aquinas' seven deadly sins are boring, as well as ugly. Envy is ugly at any age: it is hideous when it distorts an older face, and too often an older person's criticism of the young is envy in disguise. Gluttony is never becoming: it is pathetic when it is employed as a weapon to kill time. And using the sum of your years as an excuse to be lazy is to turn yourself into an emotional shut-in. Any one of the infamous seven—pride, covetousness, lust, envy, gluttony, anger, and sloth—is bad enough the first time around, but when one of them becomes a real habit it also becomes an overwhelming bore. And I found, as I went over my notes, how many of the habits of the sixties reflect these seven sins and how often they elicit boredom. Maybe you were a bore to begin with, but the years have a nasty way of enlarging the scope of your talent, opening up new territory in which you can drive your younger audiences straight up the aisle and out of the theater.

Nothing ensures an immediate attack of boredom faster than to preface a statement with "When I was young" or "Now, in *my* day." A moral point, the superiority of your conduct over today's mores, is balefully expected to follow. Stories about the old days can be entertaining if they fit into the category of human interest stories, but a sermon disguised as a reminiscence can't hide its true nature long. It's a hard truth for older people to accept—that age doesn't automatically bring wisdom in its wake. Like old veterans, we have picked up practical pointers we can (only if asked) pass on to the young recruits, but long service unfortunately doesn't guarantee great wisdom.

To say "It's my *right* to tell you what you ought to do" is to acknowledge you are on the defensive, like the would-be patriarch who said, "Anywhere I sit is the head of the table." If he felt the need to say it, he'd forfeited his place there.

If you are a grievance collector, keep your collection to yourself. Anecdotes rooted in self-pity are excruciating bores, for self-pity is a bore. Its only fascinating aspect is that if you feel sorry for yourself, nobody else feels under any obligation to feel sorry for you. You're doing too successful a job of it yourself to invite their compassion.

Have you ever by mistake put in a dress whose colors bleed with white clothes in a washing machine? Everything else in the machine is ruined, because the dye spreads so virulently. And so it is with self-pity: it can discolor anything you do or you say. A mother whose children went to visit her for a week ruined the entire seven days by sighing each morning, "Oh, it's so terrible that you can only stay a week." Which turned it into the longest week in her children's history.

In the same way you can downgrade experiences. Take the grandchildren to the seashore and say, "It's much prettier when the tide's in." Or expectations. A friend of mine was audience to an argument between a mother and her twenty-year-old son—the young man begging his mother to finance a trip to Europe the following year, the mother countering with "You can't go to Europe until you finish college." At last my friend could stand it no longer and said, "Oh, let him *want* to go to Europe!"

Arguing heatedly with younger people can be a graceless act. You don't have to agree with everything they say, but it's such a surprise for young people to find an older person who listens that if you are economical with your dissent, you have an enchanted audience when you do say something. But to try to force your viewpoint by the authority of your age is only to widen the generation gap. If someone asks you for a direct opinion on a general subject, it's a very good ploy to use the Socratic method and ask him, "Well, what do *you* think?" This does not make you, as it might seem, a complete bland blah. Quite the contrary: questioning instead of pontificating will make you a more stimulating audience. And you will be stimulated by the unexpected revelations you'll hear.

It's also delightfully disarming, when a younger person (or a contemporary, for that matter) shouts, "You're wrong," to answer, "You're right. I *am* wrong." It is a pleasing shock to hear an older person admit she is wrong, a proof that she's collected enough security in her emotional bank to afford to be wrong.

If you are that rare thing, a listener, you won't be guilty of the glazed eye that indicates you're marking time until you can leap back to *your* story. You won't, of course, ever interrupt, or anticipate what anyone is about to say. That impulse is a friendly one—it indicates that you're right in there with him, but it's cruelty to deprive him of his punch line.

You'll avoid quoting yourself. Avoid the narrative form of "And I said to the butcher . . . I told the landlord, I said. . . ."

Accept your weaknesses. If you can't remember a name, don't hold up a conversation while you fumble around or list names that *aren't* right, or say, "Now wait, it'll come to me in a minute." As a matter of fact, it's a nice conversational device to ask somebody, "Now what was the name of that person?" It makes him feel superior when he knows, which is a lovely way to make anybody feel, and then you can get on with the story. If you do have total recall, don't feature it. Don't delay another's story with "No, it was on a Thursday that she jumped off the barn, not on a Wednesday."

Avoid telling stories about your grandchildren. Of course they are cuter, smarter, funnier than any other children in the world, but screen your stories to be sure they will entertain other people. And censor the stories you tell about your children when they were young; tailor them to the listener. It may seem cute to you that your daughter, now twenty, used to say when small, "I want to go to the bandit" when she had to go to the bathroom, but it's not cute to anybody else, and it's excruciatingly embarrassing to her when the audience is her new husband.

We all could benefit from having an editor on hand to condense our family stories, and stories about our pets—and to X out all snapshots of both grandchildren and pets—and to cut out redundant phrases; older people have a dreary habit of repeating not only stories, but phrases: "It's beautiful. Perfectly beautiful." Or to cut out phrases that bring any spontaneous conversation to a grinding halt. "That's your problem" is one of them; "I never heard of him" is another.

The editor could also cut the slang or current catch-phrases. You won't hear many white-haired women say "Wow, man!" but you do hear "Hi" as a greeting, which is not becoming to them. We also have a pathetic way of not latching onto a phrase until it's as dated as "Twenty-three, skidoo." Or else we misuse it, as I found out when laughter greeted my complaint to a daughter that I was tight-up.

((15))

Gutter words are unbecoming, and distasteful to the young when we use them, for they look to older people to contribute some grace to life. That is also true of dirty stories. (I've always avoided them as I tell them badly, or don't come upon them until they are so old that they've traveled to Calcutta and back. Sex, when all passion's spent, can be funny to contemplate, but it's more prudent to laugh about it by yourself.)

We need an editor to tighten our prose, too. As you grow older, there is a tendency, in telling an anecdote, to take an awful lot of detours along the way. It's almost irresistible, especially if you are lonely and don't see people often, for when you do get a chance to talk, you talk too much. You don't really talk, you write a novel, give all the background of each character before you get to the plot. You could improve your style immeasurably by studying, on TV, the stand-up comedians. (I've yet to see a lying-down one.) Every word they use is essential and leads directly to their punch line.

Your editor would also cut constant allusions to your age: "That dates me." Well, why not? You're not passing as a young girl. "I'm an old lady but . . ." is borne in on the wings of the hope that your audience will say, "Oh, no, you're not old." All you achieve by that opener is to get people thinking about your age, when what you're aiming for is to be considered ageless.

It takes a bit of doing to accept compliments gracefully, the bittersweet kind for you, like "My, you're looking younger every day." To let go by without flinching the thoughtless remarks that sting, like the one about Walter Lippmann made to me by a middling-young man who had heard him talk at an informal meeting. "He was absolutely fascinating—kept all the other newspapermen enthralled for three hours. He was brilliant—you'd never guess that he was sixty-eight years old." It took vast control not to say, "Wait a minute. I'm sixty-seven and I'm no Walter Lippmann, but in one year from now I don't expect to fumble with the sheets, or babble of green fields."

It takes equal control for you not to consider anyone under thirty a baby, not to refer to a thirty-year-old insurance man who has irritated you as "that young pipsqueak." And to remember, when you talk to your son, that he's now a man. Forget that you once changed his diapers.

Habits can get to be insufferable bores. An example is the habit of putting "my" in front of any declaration of your next move: "Now I'm going to take *my* little nap," or "I'm going out to have *my* little walk." To telegraph your intention is in itself a bore, and is to invite when you announce, "Now I'm going upstairs and listen to *my* program," the unspoken response, "Go ahead and shut up about it."

Boring, too, is the inevitable reaction to the same stimulus, the record that clicks on when a certain name or place is mentioned. California? Your audience will hear, again, about the time you went to Los Angeles and couldn't find a single orange in the hotel's shop. Pearl Harbor? They'll hear what you were doing the exact second when the news came over the radio. Again.

It takes a special lot of doing not to be a bore when you are traveling. By all means, capitalize on your years when it comes to your luggage, which should always be kept to a minimum: look frail, and your young seat companion will offer to carry your suitcase or to flag a cab for you. But you can avoid boring others and yourself with frantic forays for supplies if you travel as a self-contained unit. When you get ready for a trip or a visit, pretend you're about to descend on the Grand Lama of Outer Mongolia and pack accordingly. Take your own supply of essential cosmetics, since there's not always a drugstore right around the corner. Take any and all of the medicines you need and the brands you like. If you're going to take a long flight to a foreign country, include your brand of laxative. The bowels have a way of reacting badly to a change of scene, and it's pretty hard to pantomime the word *laxative* to a non-English-speaking drug clerk, unless you want to be mistaken for a very low comedian.

Take an extra pair of reading glasses. If you're any kind of reader, it's disaster to break your glasses on a trip. Take your own baby pillow: hotels never have enough pillows. Take, if you smoke, a decent-sized ashtray: at hotels, and in the houses of friends who don't smoke, the ashtrays tend to be *teeny-tiny*. Pack a 100-watt bulb to replace the 25-watt number many hotels use to hold down their light bills. Take a thermos to fill with coffee or tea the night before if you are an early riser and room service doesn't open for business until 8:00 A.M.

If you plan to bring back clothes as presents for your family and friends, write down their actual measurements rather than their dress or shirt sizes. Sizing systems change with every border you cross.

If you're flying to your destination, slip a pair of bedroom slippers in the big bag you carry on the plane with you. Feet have a way of puffing up. And if your legs are long, get to the airport early enough to snag a seat on the aisle. Put a sweater or stole in your plane bag, too. It can grow cool on a plane. And if on a long flight you'd rather read than exchange complaints about in-laws with your seat companions, the $2.50 spent on earphones is a worthwhile investment. You don't have to dial in on the music or the movie, but the woman sitting next to you won't know if you don't.

Whatever your method of travel, avoid wearing a tight girdle, bra, shirt band, or belt. In your sixties the definition for bliss is taking off your girdle.

Organize your pocketbook so that you can find everything you need quickly. It's tiresome for others in line to board the plane to wait while you fumble through your bag for your ticket, muttering, "It's here *somewhere*." Carry plenty of change, and overtip. Since most bellhops and waiters expect every woman to undertip, you can shock them into giving you better service simply by doing the opposite.

When you travel with family or with friends, you have a decision to make before you set foot outside your hotel door: you can sightsee together or you can be a loner and go your own way. When you're together, there is no choice about the money involved, however. Decide who is going to be the treasurer. Give him, or her, the necessary cash, and sit back. Thus you avoid "Now, let's see, you had the avocado boat stuffed with Bimini shrimps"—"No, I had the Lucille Ball special de luxe pineapple salad." It is a routine that is the nadir of all dialogues.

If you're touring by car, you won't of course be a backseat driver. But you will be a cooperative sightseer. You will remember word games to play on the long stretches between historical monuments. If a walk of any distance is on the agenda, you don't have to be a little old lady in sneakers, but you will wear comfortable shoes so no one need listen to blister and bunion complaints. (It's a sound idea to visit a foot doctor before you leave home.) You will cheerfully face claustrophobia—and bats—to see the stalagmites and stalactites. You'll willingly pose in front of the biggest pumpkin in the world. And even if it looks like nothing else but a hunk of stone, you will lie cheerfully when the local natural formation is pointed out to you and is identified as the Crouching Camel, and say, "Why of course, anybody can see it's a camel."

Or else just skip the trip.

You will always skip giving your Treasurer's Report of how much your trip cost, item by item, as well as a course-by-course account of the meals you ate abroad.

Travelogues of these trips, whether they were jaunts to Mexico or to Newark, can have a more soporific effect on an audience than a sleeping pill. The exception is a sight or a conversation that gave a lift to your spirit or that revealed a new truth to you: a Mayan temple rising above the trees of a forest, a young veteran waiting with you for a plane's arrival who helped you understand the useless horror of Vietnam.

Your gastronomical likes and dislikes will also cause your audience to fade away as fast as they can decently do so. "I always have a bran muffin for breakfast." "I like chili, but chili doesn't like me." "Cheese binds me." Keep the gastric gossip for your doctor; it's classified material for him alone. As are stories of your operation, the diet you're on, your menopause. And your teeth are uninteresting to anyone but your dentist. Dentists are paid to be bored with your upper molar, but nobody else should be given a tour down your root canal. It's a boring trip.

The tendency as you grow older to make a David Merrick production out of an errand, which can happen to older women with not enough to do, is a crashing bore, too. I learned that from the son of a friend when he told me, "I wish Mother would get a job. It's so boring to listen to her making a day-long performance out of going to town for a loaf of bread."

This blowing up of a minor incident into a major event can be seen anytime you wait in line to return something at an adjustment counter of a store. Who is the woman raising the most hell and being the most verbose about it? It's usually a woman in her sixties, and if questioned, probably a woman without a job and often without a husband or children still under her roof.

Bad manners are ultimately the most boring things in the world. The simplest definition for bad manners is that you are thinking of yourself first. With good manners the other person comes first. The joy that good manners bring is the discovery that *other people* are fascinating. It's embarrassing to use the word *joy* unless you write the verses for Hallmark cards. But joy is the only word that can properly describe the kind of delight you discover when you listen to other people. If you stop to count, you will realize that two hands are too many to tabulate the people you know who really listen, and you will be startled to realize how much you cherish their friendship. When you yourself become a listener, you will say, with Sophocles, "Wonders are many and none is more wonderful than man," and you will not only never be a bore, you will never *be* bored for the rest of your natural life.

III

I'm Glad I Wasn't Born Beautiful

⋅⋅⋅⋅⋅⋅

Grooming is a funny word when you stop to think about it. (And one of the fringe benefits of the sixties will be time to think.) Dipping into the *American Heritage Dictionary*—more fun than into a box of chocolates and much less fattening—I found that a groom is "a man or boy employed to take care of horses." That made sense: it certainly described the way I felt about grooming when I was young, for in an era in which the majestic woman, once considered the Perfect Woman—the Lillian Russell, the Lily Langtry—had been replaced on her pedestal by the fragile woman—Queen Alexandra in England, Lillian Gish in America—I was a horse. Not a racehorse, either: more on the Percheron side. The most I could hope for was that by following the

Dictionary's next two definitions of grooming, "to clean and to brush" and "to make neat and trim," I might pass for a Shetland pony.

Big girls have an easier time of it now. Easier! Big has become the way to be. It's the small girls who now are out of fashion. It's the Ali MacGraw, big, bold, and beautiful, who is the ideal, not the Lillian Gish, fragile and defenseless. I was a big girl at the wrong time: I looked about as fragile as a Mack truck. I was pretty bitter about it and made myself sick with jealousy of my sister because it was she, not I, who had her bottom pinched in Italy, who had to fight off mashers in every country. (Mashers—*there* is another funny word.) The only man who had ever whistled at me was a truck driver who must have been as high as a kite, because the day he drove by me, an impacted wisdom tooth had swollen my face into a watermelon.

It wasn't until I began to observe and write down what made older women beautiful that I went to work to fulfill the fourth definition in the *Dictionary*—"to train, as for a specific position"—and started, like a magpie, to steal from the women who were beautiful. I first stole their assurance. Watch an accredited beauty enter a room: she makes an entrance, she floats in, on the assurance that she will be accepted as a beauty. It is obvious in her proud carriage: "She walks in beauty." Next I stole their philosophy, which they had evolved long before Bing Crosby made a popular tune of it: to accentuate the positive and eliminate the negative.

I realized I could begin by accentuating *my* positive, my hair, still a fairly cheerful tone of auburn, by wearing colors like blue and green to bring out its auburn highlights. I would eliminate the negative, the tired look of the sixties, by not challenging my face with a hairdo that shrieked *young*—a long pageboy, heavy bangs, the unruly baroque curls and falls of a *Tom Jones* wench, or, if I were black, a natural—any one of which would achieve a discordant contrast to a sixty-year-old face. And I'd skip tying my hair in a ponytail. You can't subtract the years with one, but oh, how you can add them.

I'd invest in a hair cut by an expert. I'd be careful to find one who had been kind to a friend in my age bracket (never mind the hairdresser who goes all out to make a Jackie Onassis more beautiful) and I'd ask him to cut my hair on the short side—none of those constipated little curls clustering at the back of my neck—but not too short, either. I would need all the softness I could get to minimize a wide face, and what was once a square jawline but now resembles a turtle's. I would like to have let my hair grow long so I could wear it in a bun, but with fine hair—and as one grows older hair tends to lose its body—I would look, with my hair pulled back, like a prison matron. One of the handsomest women I knew wore her hair in snoods that she crocheted in colors to match her clothes. But I can't crochet, my hair tends to dribble, and I didn't want to hear my children echo my constant admonition to my own mother, "Pin up your back hair, Ma."

Should the few gray hairs I have become the many, I won't dye my hair. (Except if I happened to have a husband or lover who was much younger than I, or a job that in this youth-oriented era forced me to lie about my age. Then I might *have* to dye my hair. But never black: a dead black creates the impression that the older woman has strayed out of a Charles Addams cartoon; and never red, which is really orange and is a brutal thing to do to an older face.) That conclusion went down in my notes the day I was wheeling my son in a baby carriage and Mary Pickford and Lillian Gish stopped to admire him. Both were about the same age, but Lillian Gish, whose neutral-colored hair softly framed her face, looked years younger than Mary Pickford, whose brass-dyed hair was vicious to her.

Nature knows a thing or two about style and especially when she chose white hair for older faces. I've been disappointed she hasn't come through yet with mine, so I could imitate my mother, who, with her white hair worn long in a French twist, had the style of a French marquise. Until she cut it short—then she was a female Mark Twain without his mustache. Women have a way of getting to look like men as they grow older, a tendency that can be minimized by feminine clothes and hairdos.

If somebody ever shocks me enough to turn my hair white overnight, I'll depend on a rinse to avoid the ugly butter-yellow that sometimes takes over the white, but I'll go easy with it, too. Nobody will identify *me* as "that blue-haired old witch."

I used to think, especially on mornings when my hair lay flat and refused to get up, that I'd love to have a wig and stop bothering with beauty parlors. This was naïve of me: wigs have to be set and washed, too; and the good ones are expensive. In a cheap wig, I'd be all set to go out trick-or-treating with my grandchildren. And I would not dare go out until the sun went down, for the cheaper, synthetic wigs, falls, and braids never match the texture of real hair, even if they make a token effort to match its color.

Wigs must be hot, too, which would cut them off my list:

yours, too, if, like me, you have an unladylike tendency to sweat. I'll leave the good wigs to the ladies who can afford to keep them up, and the feather-duster variety to Phyllis Diller. Of course, if my hair should thin out so that I might be mistaken for a bald eagle, a wig would be a necessity.

Through thick or thin, I'll brush my hair a lot—and have it cut to look as if I had just brushed it rather than called in a plumber to put it all together. I'll use only enough spray to keep it from flying off in all directions. If I can't afford to go to a beauty parlor or don't want to bother, I'll wash it often enough to keep it squeaky clean. I never want to be confused with the professional intellectual who is too busy quoting Susan Sontag to wash her hair.

Whatever color my hair becomes I'd never have it teased in any fashion. Those high, high pompadours make an older woman look, if her hair is white, as if she were a footman at the Court of Saint James; if dyed, a madam of a house, or what I imagine a madam looks like. I've yet to meet one. They may, for all I know, look like genteel ladies in reduced circumstances.

When it came to makeup, I'd use it with discretion. I'd go very easy on the rouge. Again, the most respectable older women, who have never cast a lustful eye at a man in their lives and who still think the use of lipstick would turn them into loose women, slap on enough rouge to supply a houseful of floosies.

I'd accentuate the eyebrows with a light-brown pencil or have them lightly dyed. Too much dye and I'd have two straight, stern lines on my forehead. If I had heavy eyebrows, like furry caterpillars, I'd pluck them, or have an expert go to work on them. I'd accentuate the eyes with a very modest swipe of blue eyeshadow to counteract the hooded lids that sometimes make their appearance in the sixties in both men and women. (As Noël Coward acknowledged in his self-description: "I now look like an aging Mandarin.") I would not use an eyeliner; it only focuses attention on the pouches below the eye.

I would slap on the lipstick or at least wield it with a generous hand. A lipstick in pink or rose-red, never one with yellow or orange in it. And never red-red. The cosmetic people have a name among themselves for this red-red tone: they call it "Old Lady Red." And making one application of lipstick, then one of powder, and a second serving of lipstick, guarantees my mouth will have color for a longer time. I'll remember not to chew off my lipstick. My sixties face needs it. (While I'm remembering, I'll remember not to fall into the odd habit of many women in their sixties of stretching and distorting their faces by grimacing with their lips. I see them doing it as they ride alone on the bus or subway, and I wonder if I've been at it too.)

I'll remember, too, if I do chew off my lipstick, not to do anything about it in public. A young woman making up in public can be a beguiling sight, but for an older woman to do so can be a shock, to herself most of all. Just as she thinks she is charming the birds off the trees, she is confronted with herself in her compact mirror. If she has any perspective, she may be tempted to echo Beatrice Lillie's famous rejoinder when she saw herself in a mirror: "Good God, can this be *I*?"

I'll go easy on the powder, again a powder with a pink,

not a yellow base. (Practical note: a rabbit's foot helps to distribute powder evenly.) I'll remember to powder my neck as well as my face, and watch out that I don't concentrate all the powder on my nose—a clown's trick that too many older women unwittingly imitate.

When it comes to using creams, lotions, the whole caboodle, there would seem to be something valid in the old saying that there are no ugly women, only lazy ones. I'll stipulate right here that I'm one of the lazy ones. If I had not been lazy when young, had started early on a cream and lotion regime, I'd doubtless have a flawless skin now and would be an old fool not to continue the routines. But lazy I am, and I settled long ago for a face scrub and a quick dollop of a hand cream—or that oldest of all moisturizers, rosewater and glycerine—to keep my skin soft. A soft skin is a pleasing thing for small grandchildren's hands to feel.

My casual approach means I've had to build up a gigantic sales resistance to TV commercials, for in this age, when youth has become a synonym for beauty, its pursuit is big business, an $8.5-billion-a-year business. We are exhorted, encouraged, commanded to get cracking on our appearance. We are bombarded with threats—if we don't rush out and buy X's skin cream, our husbands won't take us out to dinner; if we don't pick up Y's dye to tint our hair a madder color, our lover's eyes will stray to a blonder secretary; if we don't gobble up Z's vitamins like peanuts, our children won't give us the time of day. I resist, and settle for that dash of hand cream.

I would indulge in facials, given the time and the cash. If given enough of both, I might even try a face-lift, though I imagine at sixty-seven it's too late anyway. It would take a derrick to lift my wrinkles now. (A note of warning: a face-lift can make a face as expressionless as an egg.) I've grown accustomed to the wrinkles and sold myself that they are my service stripes. I console myself with a warning I once heard from a drama coach: "Be on your guard with people over thirty who have no crow's-feet. It means they've never laughed or cried." Because I'm still laughing and crying to beat the band, I've given up mascara and never even considered false eyelashes.

I'll have to settle (besides the hand cream) for lots of baths. Because frankly—and if I'm not frank in this chapter, we're all in trouble—we tend as we grow older to smell musty. That was the second note my grandmother contributed to my journal. It's not a horrid smell; it resembles the smell that greets you when you pull out a bureau drawer that hasn't been opened for a while. So daily baths or showers—baths for me: those sharp needles of water strike me like an invasion of privacy—are obligatory. So is toilet water, used with an extravagant hand. Not perfume, at least not the exotic, musky oriental ones that put you right in the harem, but flower scents or spicy fresh ones that make you smell as if you'd just walked by a bed of pinks early in the morning. Better forget lavender: it's an old-lady cliché.

The new freedom has made public, via TV commercials, many facets of grooming that for the normally sensitive person had better been left in the privacy of the bathroom. Of course we use deodorants! Of course we avoid clacky teeth! (I always flinch when the commercials for dentures appear on the box, inevitably while I'm eating. And why "dentures"? They're false teeth, that's what they are.) And if they move from side to side, like the keyboard of a piano, I'll get the dentist to fix them so they won't. I'll see to it too, when I first get them, that they aren't so much whiter than my original teeth that they blind my public. And, if I am unfortunate enough to have a lot of gum showing, I'll learn a new way of smiling.

Gargles to disguise bad breath? Of course I gargle before I face anyone: I smoke like a chimney, but I don't want to smell like an old cigar butt. Depilatories? Of course I shave, my legs as well as under my arms, though I don't go bare-legged anymore unless I've acquired a heavy tan on solitary days at the beach. For even if I'm one of the lucky ones who have so far escaped varicose veins, and even though, of all the anatomy, the legs are the last to go, a bare, aging leg is not a winsome sight. Nor bare feet. If I wear sandals, I won't draw attention to them with flamboyant polish on the toenails. Or highlight hands, grown pudgy, or clawlike, with a noisy-colored polish.

The only restraint shown so far in commercials is on the subject of mustaches. On women. What's holding them back? Women, some women, do have mustaches that ought to go. Even less sightly, some women have hair on their chins. Unless they are stand-ins for Macbeth's witches, they'd better do something about it, and quick. They might check on the nostrils and the ears, too, while they're about it.

Just because I'm lazy and broke doesn't mean I'm putting down all cosmetics. Filthy-rich, I'd have a shelf crowded with sweet-smelling creams and astringents. I'm not convinced they'd make me the beauty I always wanted to be, or if I had been beautiful, put me back in flower again, but they'd make me *feel* prettier. As things, and I, now stand, though, I'll have to count on happiness to do the trick. It can do it, every time. It did it for me a few months ago, when after my publisher telephoned to say they wanted me to write this book, I flew into my daughter's office, and before I could say a word she cried, "Ma, what have you done to yourself? You look about forty!"

Hope is a great facial, too. Hope is the beauty treatment that makes young faces beautiful: they expect that something wonderful is waiting for them right around the corner. The best potion of all is love, just as hate is the worst. It is not laughter that etches the lines around your mouth; it is hate that digs the ditches there. Look again at the older women who are beautiful. They may no longer look like swans, supercilious and remote, and their features may be blurred, but their love of life is there, a glow that all the chemists at Lizzie Arden's can't enhance, that all the years can't extinguish.

IV

That Dress Is You

❦☙

The most expensive dress I've ever owned was bought with a friend's advice. It didn't cost the most, but it was the most expensive because I never wore it unless everything else was at the cleaner's. I can still see it, though it has been years since it went to the Salvation Army to cover some luckless back. It was a shiny silk dress in phlegm gray with a jacket that hit me at the widest spot, my hips, and it made me feel like a confidential secretary who for thirty years had denied herself lovers, husbands, and children to become the perfect office wife to the president of the International Bank for String Savings. I hated it.

It was expensive, too, because of the vast sums spent in futile attempts to better its condition: bright scarves and necklaces bought to relieve its severity and—after spending money at a tailor's to convert the dress into a skirt—white blouses to give it that fresh look. Nothing worked. And, perversely, it refused to be the victim of an accident; the favorite dress gets the Clorox spilled on it, never the hated one.

I should have known better than to take a friend shopping with me. I had once been the saleswoman who completed that tense triumvirate of customer, friend, and saleswoman that crowds a fitting room. As in the Vip cartoon of the two men walking down the street laughing as one says, "If looks could kill, eh, Ed?" while in the background a figure lies prone on the sidewalk, I would have, if I could have, killed my customer's friend with a look. For at the critical moment when, with gentle persuasion, I had deflected her interest from a flaming red dress that made her look like an over-blown peony, to a becoming blue one, her friend inevitably would stop contemplating herself in the mirrors long enough to say, "Tony-really-gave-me-a-lousy-haircut-this-time-take-the-red-one."

Next to friends and family, your greatest shopping enemy is the saleswoman who has not only kissed the Blarney stone, but swallowed the damn thing, who fuzzes your judgment with the triumphant cry "That dress is *you!*" when all three mirrors in the fitting room testify to its only being you if you have thrown in the towel forever.

Your best ally is the saleswoman who knows you, the price you can pay, and the lines, materials, and colors that enhance you. That *you* feel enhance you. If you're lucky, or patient enough to find her, never let her go.

You will have better luck finding her in specialty shops or

in the more expensive departments of larger stores. Maybe, if you're naturally chicken like me (do you find yourself saying "I'm sorry" to the prerecorded voice on the phone when it tells you that you've dialed the wrong number?) you will tend to avoid an encounter with the salesladies there, with their haughty "Yes, madame?" greeting that translated means "You are in the wrong department, my good woman; the basement is three flights down." For years, they made me feel as if I were back barefoot in the Ozarks, until the time came when I needed them. Then I sailed in like a proud ship, told them the truth about what I wanted and how much I had to spend for it, and the truth *did* set us free, free to be human together.

And if, again like me, you find that your sixties have brought in their wake a set income that's set on a very small scale, you *will* need the help of these ladies, because more than ever before you are going to need expensive clothes. Not so many of them as in your more golden days, but what you do buy has to be made of expensive material, has to have the line and fit that can be found only in expensive clothes. Because in the sixties you need all the help that good material and good line can give you. And because, once it's bought, you will be wearing whatever you buy until it lies down and cries uncle.

Even if you are as rich as fudge, you would be wise, before you set foot outside the door, to follow up on the Greek adage and know thyself—thyself as thee is *now*. Look at yourself in a full-length mirror, and if you haven't one, you are, I regret to tell you, a moral coward. It may turn out to be your first sock in the eye, but it's a direct way of easing into the harder sock—*who* you are. Take everything you have out of your closets and your bureaus, try everything on, keep only what you feel confident in, and call the Salvation Army to come for the rest. That takes daring, but the sixties are no time for timidity.

You have probably already chosen the personality in her sixties whose style you would like to adapt and have checked current fashions for styles that will fit the role you've chosen (unless you've chosen to be Whistler's Mother, a distinguished way to look if you have the guts to carry it off). To choose and adapt should be no new concept to you. You have doubtless always chosen among the current fashions the ones that most became you and rejected the ones that didn't. (I'll bet the thirties didn't put an Empress Eugenie hat on *your* head.)

But there is a different slant to your choices now that you are sixty. There is the obligation to be kind to yourself, to look for the lines and colors that are kind to you. Now is the hour to flatter and deceive, not to reveal. Chic should give way to prettiness. Pretty is an unfashionable word today, but a pretty woman is never out of fashion. I don't know your definition of pretty; I hope it doesn't connote a busy, busy look of baubles, bangles, and beads, that it does mean pretty as an English garden is pretty: fresh and serene in the early morning light. Serenity is the word for the sixties.

So, secure in the knowledge of what you want, you set out to shop. And bang! You run smack into the enemy before you can unbutton your coat. I was wrong about the flattering saleswoman; she is not your greatest enemy. Seventh Avenue is, where the clothes they sell are dreamed up. The manufacturers there have drunk so deep at the Fountain of Youth that it's a wonder they don't make their sales

pitch in baby talk. If you doubt it, look at the current adver-
tisements, note the size ranges (a 16 is a rarity), watch the
commercials on television, and you will be convinced that if
you are over thirty you are not as good as dead, you would
be *better* dead. *Women's Wear Daily*, the official voice of
Seventh Avenue, makes no bones about it; with cynical
frankness, they call all of us over thirty-five "the Forgotten
Women."

Which would seem to leave us only two choices. The
first is to buy the clothes they've decreed are suitable for the
sixties: the serviceable, shapeless drab coat, the dress with
the sweetheart neckline (you're nobody's sweetheart when
you wear one, but you do look like a lady in reduced circumstances—a pathetic sight). The other is to choose the
way-out fashions that make us parodies of the young, which
is a grotesque sight, as well as pathetic. It's the back of their
hand to anybody over thirty-five and over size 12 who has
any taste. Seventh Avenue seems to work on the principle
that as you gain in years or pounds, you lose your taste. Unless you are rich, rich. Then you can escape the dictatorship
of Seventh Avenue by taking your rich, rich checkbook,
now that Mainbocher has retired, to George Stavropoulos,
the young Greek designer whose elegant clothes, like Mainbocher's, are as dateless as a flower.

But wait! Wait! Don't give way to despair! If you aren't
rich, there's still hope. You *can* bypass Seventh Avenue's
power to make you either pathetic or grotesque, if you
know what you want and where and when to look for it.

You can be on the lookout for clearance sales. They can
prove worth your while, especially if you have established a
saleswoman as an ally in the store. And if you know a good

thing when you see it. Some stores have a tricky ploy: they buy up the dogs (the trade's name for the models that didn't make the grade) and add them to the racks of their own reduced stock. The tip-off on them is the sight of one style represented by five or six dresses or coats in each size.

You will also find a goodly crowd of clothes on the sale racks with labels that read MADE IN ITALY (OR FRANCE) ESPECIALLY FOR . . . followed by the name of the store. It would be a far, far better thing for you if the label read "BEWARE!" for too many clothes from across the seas have very peculiar proportions, maybe because women in other countries are shaped differently from American women, maybe because European designers *think* American women are shaped differently from their women. Whatever the reason, take care; give yourself a long, long look in the mirrors before you buy.

Sales are most rewarding if you don't go with a rigid notion of what you hope to find. If you are determined to buy a wool jersey in emerald green or nothing, not only may you be disappointed, you may miss the dress in a color or fabric that you've never thought of but that could give you unexpected pleasure for a long time. (It's reasonable to avoid colors or designs that are currently the craze, for they will date the dress.)

Don't leave at home, though, the image of what you want to look like. You will never, just because the price is right, want to settle for anything that doesn't enhance the woman you have decided to be. Look for your own personality, not for a bargain.

Be wary of the one-day sales, the Lincoln's Birthday and Columbus Day sales—the dogs are barking there, too.

Often there are better bargains to be found in the better departments of a store all during the year. Again, it helps if you have a salesperson there who is on your side and willing to call or to tell you about the best buys.

Take time at sales. Another reason to shop alone: nobody is holding a table for you and your friend at Schrafft's. If a saleswoman tries to hurry you out of the fitting rooms—which are at a premium during sales—tell her firmly to go away. For you can no longer afford mistakes; you need clothes that will reflect a remark of Louis XV, "It will last my time." The days of impulse buying are as far away now for you as the days of wine and roses, or are restricted to the little things: the wild scarf to brighten a gray day, the knitted cap to wear when you walk the dog in the winter dusk.

You will, of course, never think of buying anything without trying it on. Finding your size in a style you like is a hollow victory when you try it on at home, find it won't work, and have to return it. (If you *can*. Some stores take the sign ALL SALES FINAL seriously.) Sizing, unfortunately, is not standardized; a size 12 in an inexpensive dress could be a 10 in a better dress. And in cheaper clothes, there is no fabric wasted on generous seams or hems that can be let out.

It's a sound idea to go to sales—or to do any clothes shopping, for that matter—the day before you get your hair fixed or the day after you stayed up late to see an old Robert Montgomery movie. For if you like what you see in the mirror when your hair is a nest of robins and the lines around your eyes could double for a topographical map of Tibet, you'll be crazy about yourself when you feel fat and sassy again.

If you *are* fat, or if you're still protecting your ego with the euphemism "slightly overweight," don't sell yourself on a dress by thinking, "It will look great when I lose ten pounds." It's better to get a dress too loose than too tight: a tight one reveals the bulge over your bra in the back, and in the front, if it's a buttoned-down style, it gapes. Buy for the way you look now. What good is a new dress waiting in the closet for the day you go back to lettuce and grapefruit?

Occasionally, in sports-clothes departments especially, you can find a dress or suit that will be a friend to you if you spend money on alterations. At first glance, it seems absurd to advocate adding ten or twelve dollars in alterations to a $19.95 buy. It looked absurd to the saleswoman who sold me a blue denim suit for $22.95 last summer when I added $15.00 to its cost to have the shoulders narrowed and the skirt let out over the hips and lengthened. (For, like many over-sixty figures, mine now calls for one size from the waist up, another from the waist down.) But the $15.00 transformed the suit into one of the treasures in my closet, for it joined the ranks of the ones I reach for most.

Fat or thin, be wary about ordering clothes from an ad you've seen in a newspaper or magazine. The girls who model them are usually suffering malnutrition from their diet of bloody Marys and B12 shots. The stylist from the advertising agency has outfitted them for the photograph with bags, shoes, and jewelry worth a hundred times the price of the dress. The highest-paid fashion photographer has flown them (along with Kenneth to fix their hair) to Greece, posed them against the pillars of the Acropolis, and turned up his wind machines high to send their skirts floating in the wind. If you want to avoid the let-down of seeing yourself in an unbecoming light, and the boring chore of finding the wrapping paper, string, and label necessary to return what you ordered, you'd do well before you write for it to visualize yourself in the photographed dress, leaning against the shelf of Lemon Pledge in your supermarket.

Boutiques have sprung up on the fashion landscape in the last few years like bizarre flowers. You may be able to find a skirt or shirt in one for your moments of madness, but boutiques are essentially expensive flowers and for those whose year *is* at the spring.

More worth exploring are the resale shops. In New York, they are where women on or aspiring to be on the list of the ten best-dressed women, actresses, and TV personalities take their last season's clothes for resale. Again, if you go alone and with plenty of time on your hands, you can find real gems there. (Don't be put off by the idea of the clothes being secondhand. Legitimate resale shops won't accept anything for resale that hasn't been cleaned and that hasn't got all its buttons.) If you live in a smaller town and are naturally reluctant to face a bridge partner in the dress she sent for resale to your local Junior League shop, take a drive to a neighboring town or suburb and explore *its* resale shop.

The most effective instrument to use against Seventh Avenue is a sewing machine. I'm not talking about a back-to-the-little-dressmaker movement (and why are they always called little?). Dressmakers are hard to find today; most of them, defeated by high rents, have gone to work in the alterations departments of stores. If you do find one, her prices will probably be astronomical. I'm talking about *you* sitting down at your own sewing machine.

I don't want to foment a revolution that will put the quarter of a million people who earn their living on Seventh Av-

enue out of work—but I don't have to. Seventh Avenue itself has already started things rolling. With high prices and
with unbecoming fashions, it is driving women back to sewing. Proof? Some statistics: 44 million homes now have sewing machines, 2 million sewing machines are sold every
year, 25 percent of all dresses worn are homemade. *Harper's
Bazaar* has introduced home sewing as a regular subject in
all its issues.

It makes sense: a chemise dress that would cost $35.00 to
$45.00, if bought from Seventh Avenue by way of a depart-
ment store, can be run up at home for $8.00 to $9.00. *I*
couldn't run it up—with my fear of anything mechanical, or
rather, mechanical things' hostility to me, a sewing machine
would reach out and hemstitch *me*—but I'm lucky enough
not to have to even try. When I turned fifty, I made two
resolutions for the day I hit sixty: I'd have a dog, and I'd
never again wear a dress with a belt. I was able to fulfill both
resolves when a friend gave me Peakie and another friend,
whose business was transferred from New York to Japan,
volunteered to have my unconventional beltless shifts made
there, in beautiful materials for practically no money.

But if I weren't an overage Tokyo Rose, I would be
tempted to learn to sew at one of the adult classes given at
YWCA's or at Singer Sewing Machine Centers or, here in
New York, at the French Fashion Academy. There, so a
friend tells me, she learned in eight hours of study to make
slacks that would be $29.95 in stores, for $8.00. And they
fit. I'd take a graduate course in tailoring, too, to cope with
armholes and zippers.

Then I wouldn't have to wait for the mail from Japan or
go naked until Seventh Avenue wakes up to the fact that the

forgotten women are a forgotten market that could bring it more money. All of us over sixty could form a protest march up Seventh Avenue, carrying our homemade banners: "We don't *all* listen to Lawrence Welk!" "*We* never screamed at Liberace!" We could storm the ramparts (as soon as we put on our bifocals to find them) and chant together our marching song, "The back of our hands to *you*!"

V

Dresses for Breakfasts, and Dinners, and Balls

❧❦❧

Dresses for breakfasts, and dinners, and balls;
Dresses to sit in, and stand in, and walk in;
Dresses to dance in, and flirt in, and talk in;
Dresses in which to do nothing at all;
Dresses for Winter, Spring, Summer, and Fall.*

I'm not as uninhibited as my mother, who once startled a girl sitting on a front porch by shouting to her as we drove by in our Model T Ford, "Pull down your skirt!" But I am so astonished by the cruel things I see women do to themselves with the clothes they wear that I catch myself saying out loud on the street, "Oh, *no*! Never!"

"Dressed to please, not to astonish" is a wise maxim for the sixties. An eighty-year-old woman said it, Coco Chanel, whom a *New York Times* headline called "the fashion spirit of the twentieth century." She knew what she was talking

* From "Nothing to Wear," by William Allen Butler (*Harper's Weekly*, February 7, 1857)

((44))

about—had known ever since the end of World War I, when she was an instant success with chemise dresses and suits whose easy lines reflected accurately the escape of women from passive to active roles. Her clothes still do, another proof that while fashions change, style is constant. "The most important thing to remember about fashion," she also said, in a November, 1970, interview with *Women's Wear Daily*, "is that it isn't always right to be in fashion"—a line to cheer us who are in the sixties, who have found there the wisdom to realize we no longer have to compete. We don't have to join, like lemmings, the hysterical race after the latest fashion nonsense. We have arrived at our place in the scheme of things: we have chosen our own style of nonsense, and we are content with it.

Chanel followed her own convictions: in the same interview with *Women's Wear* (the edition was given over to plugging long skirts), she said, "I've photos of myself taken twenty years ago and my skirts were the same length then as they are now." It takes a woman of conviction to defy fashion; it may strengthen yours to resist the dress designed with a sixteen-year-old in mind if you realize that in it you would astonish, but the astonishment you would evoke would not be based on admiration but would make you a recipient for what Chanel called "the glance without pity."

Here are some tips culled from my "Oh, *no!* Never!" notes. It may seem as presumptuous to list what you should wear as to tell you whom you should like, but considered as traffic signs, the tips may shorten your trips through the stores and add to your pleasure in the wearing of the choices you made there.

Your choices will be determined, of course, by a variety of ingredients: what your sixties figure is like, where you will wear the dress, when you will wear it, and, if your spirit is free but your money limited, how long you can wear it. Look for a dress that pleases *you*, for if you are pleased with yourself, you will please your public. Look, above all, for a dress that is kind to you, that makes no big demands of you.

You may be one of the lucky ones who can wear the same size at sixty that you wore at twenty, but you would be wise not to wear the same lines that you did then. For instance, if you have the same waist measurement, don't emphasize it with a gaucho belt above a full skirt, for who wants to look like the oldest ballerina still vertical? Fat or skinny, tall or short, in the city or in the country, in winter or summer, make it easy on yourself. Be kind to the five areas of your figure that in your sixties need all the help you can give them.

Let's start at the top, with your neck. And let's be honest—nobody is going to compare it to a swan's now that it is ringed with wrinkles that you cannot hide; though some try, as you know when you remember the news photos of Hope Hampton as she swept down the aisle on opening night at the opera, swathed up to her eyeballs in yards of tulle. But you can avoid necklines that are demanding, such as the stark V neckline or the unrelieved cardigan, and can look instead for a dress with a draped neckline, a club or a round collar (leave the top button unbuttoned for a softer line) or a rolled one. Even the V and the cardigans are possible, if amenable to scarves.

A dress with a scarf woven in and out of tabs made of the

same material as the dress is a good idea if you can sew; they aren't easy to find in stores. A high neck, referred to as a jewel neckline in the ads, is good, too, if you take the jewel part of it literally and wear pearls—a sixties banality, to be sure, but a sound one, for they add that element of white that is an invaluable flatterer close to your face. Be sure the neckline is cut to hug the back of your neck to cover another sixties hazard, the dowager's hump. For the same reason, avoid conspicuous buttons that march up the middle of your back.

Cast a jaundiced eye on any buttons, especially buttons on pockets placed at the breast line—or rather where the breast line is supposed to be. One of the harsher socks in the eye to be faced at sixty is that the breasts have fallen, and while a properly fitted bra will prevent their meeting up with your waistline, it will not duplicate the sweet high breasts of spring. If you force them higher by a tighter bra, you don't fool anybody. Jamming the breasts up together where they no longer belong will achieve not a sexy look but rather an unsavory facsimile of a bowl of wrinkled prunes. Better leave the cleavages to Raquel Welch. Leave her the breast pockets as well, for a breast nestling below a pocket is not to be contemplated.

Another area that calls for T.L.C. is the arm, the part of the body the years are most ruthless to. They leave it pretty much alone from the elbow down—they can't do much further harm to the elbow, since except for a baby's elbow, it is no thing of beauty to begin with—but they are vicious to the upper arm. If thin, the years turn it into a stick; if fat, into a pink balloon. But that's not the worst: fat, thin, or just right everywhere else, there's no escaping that flabby roll that shakes with every move your arm makes. It's a dirty trick the years play, but you're stuck with it.

The only retaliation is to put your upper arm into hiding for the duration—with long or three-quarter-length sleeves, the first line of defense and the most flattering; if hips have widened, longer sleeves also help to balance their width. (Practical note: have the store or a tailor put in—or if you can sew, put in yourself—a patch inside the sleeves at the elbow; it will obviate the risk of your being out at the elbows before you've worn out the dress. And a panel inside the back of the skirt will prevent the butt-sprung look.)

Think twice about very full, heavily decorated, or ruffled sleeves. If you are short, they will pull you down to the ground; if tall, strike fear in your public that any minute you may lean against a piano and belt out, "There are fairies in the bottom of my garden." During the long hot summers you can compromise with short sleeves—even a cap sleeve is better than no sleeve at all. *Anything*—a stole of cool material, a cotton sweater or jacket thrown over your shoulders—is better than no sleeves, for as well as that horrendous roll of fat on the arms, there is that other roll of flab to contend with that pops up under the armpit in a sleeveless dress, another roll that must never be allowed to see the light of day.

Fashion has been kind enough to give us the answer to another hazard—the widening hips and thickening waist. It gave us the shift, which is easy to wear as well as becoming. If cut loose, it hides the hips and you don't have to hold in your stomach. When I was young, I used to wonder why so many older women looked pregnant. "He jests at scars, that never felt a wound." I don't wonder anymore.

The shift is such a relaxed as well as a becoming style, it would seem to be the inevitable choice for one's sixties. However, if you still have a waist, or more important, if you *feel* better in a fitted dress, the shirtdress is your dish, along with its kissin' cousin, the coatdress. It has been around for a long time, gives no indication of ever leaving. Its simple lines and its adaptability to any fabric, any situation, have won for it the accolade of a classic. Mme Pompidou, the French president's wife, wore a lavender silk one to a White House lunch; Claudette Colbert's dress for a top-drawer movie bash was a shirtdress in white chiffon; the most elegant mother of the bride I ever saw wore at a summer wedding a shirtdress in sand-colored raw silk. With her plain, wide, sand-colored Milan hat, she turned the gussied-up guests there into a twittering crowd of Barbie dolls. In velvet or in denim, at a supermarket or at a command performance, the shirtdress is always blue chips. (Practical note: if your waist has thickened, a belt in the same material is better than one in contrasting material or color. Or if you hanker for leather, let it be suede, rather than a shiny leather.)

A two-piece dress, a dress with a matching jacket or bolero, is also a sixties banality, but again, if you feel comfortable in it that's reason enough to wear one. Avoid the jacket that ends smack at the widest part of your hips; settle for either the bolero that stops just above your waistline or the longer jacket that comes well down on your hips. (Practical note: if you opt for a dress with a bolero, have weights sewn inside at the back, since it's as well to avoid the bolero that rides up at the back as you fill it out in the front.)

The last of the danger areas is the knees, with special attention needed to the back of the knees. Like elbows, few knees have inspired sonnets. (Ann Pennington, a dancer in the Ziegfeld Follies way back when, was known for her "Bee's Knees," a phrase that baffled me then, and now.) Your skirt length should eliminate the hazard of their being seen. The lengths of skirts, of course, go up and go down. Still, whatever the current fashion, you won't want to wear your skirts at a length that will stop traffic, and by now you have probably settled on a length that makes you feel most at ease, because it is in proper proportion to your figure.

The A-line is the best of all lines for your skirts. A straight skirt will reveal more than you want anybody to know—the hipbones if you're skinny, the bulges if you're fat, and, viewed from the back, the shape of your buttocks. Contrary to accepted rules, a pleated skirt can be flattering to a larger figure if the pleats are concentrated in the back and front, the skirt flat on the hips. (If it's not flat to begin with, it can be altered.) If you have more hip than you like, it's a good notion to take out the pockets and sew up their openings. You won't want to put your hands in your pockets, anyway, for you'll only wear out the material surrounding them. And standing legs apart, hands in pockets, is a gamine's caper. And as long as you've given up the little-girl look, with its kittenish ruffles and bows, you must have long since shed the gamine look, too.

You have doubtless already discovered that, with patience and a pair of comfortable shoes, it is easier to find a dress with lines that please you in wool than in silk or synthetics, and without having to sell your engagement ring. But if, on a prowl for cool dresses for summer, you do find one, give a close look to the fabric. Some synthetics, especially those in

linen or shantung weave, can turn out to be as hot as the
torture box Alec Guinness endured in *The Bridge on the
River Kwai.* Pure silk, hard to find in this era of man-made
fabrics, is deliciously cool, but musses with one sitting,
which is nothing to hold against it if you don't mind ironing.
Linen, real Irish linen, is cool and cool-looking, but brings
the same ironing chore with it. Cotton is almost always a
good alternative, since it is nowhere near as crushable as
linen. Sheers? In dark colors, the slip underneath is more
prominent than the dress; in light colors, they belong at a
garden party that even the queen of England wouldn't be
caught dead at.

Don't waste one moment's glance at Arnel jerseys, either
in plain colors or in prints: they cling, and Q.E.D., they are
the cruelest fabric you could pick. They must be stamped
out, year after year, by a bunch of boys who hate their
mothers. Never is their mother hang-up more apparent than
in the prints they cut for the Mom-trade: the tags on these
dresses should carry the identifying label THE SON'S RE-
VENGE.

Some of the blame belongs on Mom's shoulders, for she
buys them, amazing as it seems, on the principle that "a
print does something for me." It does—it does something
horrendous. Most of the prints available to her affront the eye
with frantic designs: psychedelic-colored whirlpools, June
bustin' out all over in cabbage roses meant to bloom on
sofas, or cute patterns that would have charmed Walt Dis-
ney but nobody else—pink poodles or blue kittens chasing
each other 'round and 'round the widening plains.

Beautiful prints *do* exist: clean, small geometric designs,
stripes (they had better be vertical; in horizontal ones you

might be mistaken for a child's whirling top), paisleys, small
flowers in refreshing clear colors, discreet polka dots to enhance the tranquil, uncluttered look that so becomes the
sixties. But they are not easy to find at reasonable prices or
in reasonable sizes for the sixties. So, unless you can conform to a gilded Palm Beach woman's philosophy, which
she set down in needlepoint on a cushion, "You can't be too
rich or too thin," you may have to get to that sewing machine.

Dresses for evening are easier to come by. They may, in
this more casual age, be an academic need. As for that dated
category, the cocktail dress, thank your lucky stars it *is*
dated. It was a fussy, tacky idea to begin with; a simple,
beautifully cut dress in silk or lightweight wool was always
more at ease at parties and never threatened its wearer with
the most uncomfortable of all sartorial crises: being over-
dressed. But you'll feel safer if you have one dinner dress
hanging in your closet if it's not there already, for how can
you foresee your future? There may be a prize in it for you,
and what would you have to wear to the presentation dinner?

It's too bad for the sixties set that people don't dress more
in the evenings, for in an evening dress a woman in her
sixties is *en fleur*. Her poise can carry off rich fabrics, draped
jerseys, even black lace—if it's real lace—as long as the fabric is not shiny. She'll leave satin and organza to the brides,
the Empire line to the young, and lamé to Lena Horne.
She'll skip velvet, too, if she's to have only one evening
dress: it looks dusty in the summer, and its nap gets too
shiny too fast where she sits down. There are short dinner
dresses all around, but why shouldn't she have the pleasure

of making a grand entrance in a long one? She'll avoid sequins, fringes, and feathers: furbelows that take a Marlene Dietrich to carry off, and *she* put in quite a few years converting herself from a pudgy hausfrau into a woman who could get away with them.

Finding dresses for night and for day will be easier if you look for the lines and the colors that have brought from your audience the most satisfying kind of applause—the comment not "what a pretty dress" but "how pretty you look." If you look for dresses that please *you*, because they give you confidence that you look as well as it is possible for you to look, then you will have achieved the ultimate purpose of clothes. That is my answer to the tiresome old question, whom do women dress for? If they have the sense that God gave geese, they dress for the confidence that the right clothes give them, and they wear clothes that fit the best description I ever heard of the right kind of dress. In answer to a question from the hairdresser, "What are you going to wear to the party?" the woman sitting next to me at the beauty parlor one day said, "I have a very good-looking dress I've had for ages. Whenever I don't know what to wear, I wear it. And I feel fine."

VI

Red Does Something for You

It's too bad that Joan Crawford has exchanged her role of movie queen for that of woman executive. I always used to anticipate the annual feature about her in the movie magazines at the beauty parlor invariably titled "The New Joan Crawford." For each year she shucked off her image of the year preceding to emerge with a new philosophy of life and a new hairdo.

No movie magazine may feature your transformation, but you'd do well to consider your choice of colors to wear in the light of "The New You." And in the harsh light of an overhead lamp. You may be in for a shock. The self-deception that believes the lie is endemic to most older women:

they think of themselves as looking always as they looked at about forty. Look again. You're sixty. The chances are good (or bad) that your alabaster skin has turned sallow. Or that, even if it hasn't, you look tired. You're not tired. You're sixty, and all the perfumes of Arabia or the creams of Lizzie Arden can't sweeten the weary look.

But kind colors can minimize it. Colors are usually divided into two categories: warm or cool. For us in our sixties it's more helpful to think of them as kind or cruel. To be kind they had better be clear rather than muddy and soft rather than harsh.

Black, contrary to tradition, is not for senior citizens. (There is a gruesome phrase! It must have been concocted by a government P.R. man named Portnoy.) Black is a depressant. It needs the fresh complexion of the young to carry it off, with two exceptions. It can be becoming in evening clothes, when bright lights and soft music bring a glow to an older face. And it can be becoming in the daytime with the addition of white or a light shell pink, in the print of a dress or of a scarf. Don't waste time, though, looking for the good little black dress. It's not good anymore. It's an unimaginative bore.

Next to black, brown is the cruelest color. A warm nut brown, in a coat or suit, worn against a country background, can please, but it is only kind if it is sparked by another color, a light-blue scarf or one of cherry red. All browns tend to look serviceable and therefore dull.

For a basic color, navy is the kindest to the sixties. It has some life in it that is missing in black. But it has its dangers, too. If zest isn't added to it by the introduction of a strong second color—shocking pink, jade, yellow (a lemon, not a buttery yellow)—you run the risk of being mistaken for your maiden aunt. The bravely indigent one.

The blue spectrum is a friendly one for you: bright navy; the gray-blue shade once called French, now air-force blue; powder blue. Aqua is gentle, too, if the tone has been softened with white. A true aqua is as hard as rocks. So is royal blue—it is the hardest, and anyway it's a tacky color. Forget, if you ever contemplated it, the blue that is called on color charts Prussian blue but, because of its insistent appearance in half-size dresses, should be called menopause blue.

You'd do well to forget gold, rust, and orange: only youth can survive their noisy statements. Mustard and avocado have their dangers, too. They are muddy colors, not for you.

Gray, like black, used to be a traditional little-old-lady color. No more. But little or big old ladies will find a dove gray more becoming than the darker tones because, again, it has white in it. Charcoal gray can have great style, but a somber effect if not relieved by a clear color. That's also true of the tans and the beiges—and you need to watch what styles they are made up in. A shirtdress in beige can turn you into an aging airline stewardess, a belted coat in khaki into an overage spy. Like black and brown, gray or beige had better never meet your neck. It should always be the kindest color for you there: plain white, or shell pink.

White can be a staunch friend. And an expensive one, to keep white. Watch out for the all-white summer dress—the passerby may expect to hear you say, "Take this and rinse out your mouth, please."

Hunter green, as a basic color, is an unsung friend, which is a shame, because it is a kind color with great style. Apple green is bland, but cool-looking for summer and in the country. Jade green has a bravado it will pass on to you.

So has red—as a sparkler to a serene color. Even as a sparkler, it had better have plenty of blue in it: be a rosy red, never a Christmas red. Santa Claus may be a jolly old elf, but Santa Claus red is Scrooge himself to the sixties. Wine isn't cruel, but is apt to look sad. Purple *is* cruel, plum is kind. A clear lavender has style, a grayed lavender will set you down square in the rocking chair.

Dresses in black, brown, navy, gray, or a beige that's nudging cream are a pleasant surprise to see on a hot day in the city. Pastels look cool, if they are made up in city styles. Too relaxed or too fussy, they make you look as if you should be singing, "It's so peaceful in the country," and should be in the country proving it. A pastel wool worn in the winter is as good as a shot of B12 for your spirits. I've never figured out why houses in tropical climates are painted pastel colors, while the ones in northern climates are in dreary grays and browns. A reversal, a pink house seen on a sodden February day, would be a great spirit-lifter.

To be a black woman is to have a far greater latitude in your choices of color. You can continue to wear the shades you've always enjoyed. I hope you haven't enjoyed the neutrals too much. The grays, browns, navies, and blacks are such a waste: you're throwing away the handsome contrast that you could achieve of strong tones or vibrant pastels against your dark skin.

If you are fat, you'll feel more confident in the less strident colors. A fat woman in a bright red dress is as noisy as a brass band. In a psychedelic green she shrieks like chalk on a blackboard.

If "imprisoned in every fat man a thin one is wildly signaling to be let out," it's equally true that in every older woman there is a young woman who still wants to be seen. And if you happened to wear a red dress the night your husband proposed, it's no surprise that you still want to wear red. But beware: with skin now muddied by the years, you may be playing a mean trick on yourself.

However, if your husband likes you in red, the hell with all my suggestions. He is the audience you want to please, so all bets are off. You can cheat a little, though. You can keep red for a spectacular robe to wear at home and never have to face the rest of your audience looking like a beefsteak tomato. And the chances are worth the gamble that though your husband has indicated he likes you in red, when you are dressed in a color *you* feel happy in, that one will become his favorite color for all time.

VII

Well-Suited for the Sixties

Four coats? The new role I'd chosen for my sixties self demanded *four* coats? It was a shocking number. It staggered me until courage returned with a close examination of the three already hanging in the closet, all in shape to fight the good fight for at least one more year.

The minimum of four—a winter dressed-up coat, a spring-fall dressed-up coat, a winter casual coat, a spring-fall casual coat—was determined by the role I was about to create: that of a Mrs. Longworth, disguised as a sixty-seven-year-old free-lance writer who had a dog, who lived in a big city, who snapped at any invitations for a weekend in the country. Being a free-lance writer meant I would have to be a saleswoman, and the product I would be selling was me;

the most effective pitch would be to look as if I didn't need the work. To carry out that deception, I would have to wear my best dress when I went hustling, and a best dress called for a best coat. Since I would be first hitting the pavement in the winter, a winter dressed-up coat was needed. It would be my biggest investment since it couldn't be a cheap coat for two reasons: a cheap coat *looks* cheap, and it wouldn't have the long life that is the fringe benefit of an expensive coat.

I'd be careful not to get one in a color that would soon be a bore. A coat in a strident color, a flaming red or a violent green, would be a spirit-lifter on a gray day, and so pleasant to own if I had other coats, but with only one dressed-up one it could grow to be as abrasive as Professor Higgins' mother-in-law, "with a voice that shatters glass." The same stricture would restrain me from a coat in a bold tweed, even a tweed with an urban cut to its jib. A coat in a pastel color would look as if I should be in Palm Beach, and I would run up big cleaning bills—unless I married the cleaner.

A navy or black, gray or sand, brown, dark green, plum, or perhaps a muted combination was what I must find—or a tweed or tattersall, herringbone or check with a quiet look about it. And I must remember, if I chose a plaid or check, that red and blue together look like purple; red and yellow, like orange.

Which neutral I chose would be predicated on what dresses I had. Thank goodness, we are much freer now about mixing colors than when I was young: we wear black with brown, gray with black. But black with navy has a defeated look; so has gray with navy. When I do find the right

neutral coat, I must remember to counteract its neutrality
with a wild scarf or hat. If I were rich I'd try for the ultimate in elegance and have everything—coat, hat, dress,
shoes, bag—the same color, but without each component
being elegant on its own, all I would achieve would be the
compulsively neat look of an English nanny.

I wouldn't go to the other extreme and get a sloppy coat
without buttons that I'd have to clutch closed. The sleeves
of the coat would have generous armholes, or the kimono
sleeves of my dresses would take a terrible beating. Padded
shoulders went out with Norma Shearer, but I'd avoid the
dropped shoulder or the dolman sleeve: I need a squarish
look up top to balance my hipline. I'd check that there was a
generous hem. I might want to match the length of my
dresses with the current waterline in fashions—my courage
is not so high as Chanel's—and I wouldn't want the dreary
look of a dress showing below my coat. And I'd be sure to
walk around the store a bit in the coat before I bought it,
long enough to discover if it weighed me down, for a heavy
coat can be a real burden to carry. Like a blanket, a coat
doesn't have to be heavy to keep you warm.

If I couldn't find a discreet tweed, I'd look for a coat in a
flannel or basket weave. I wouldn't choose a practical material, like a hard-woven pepper-and-salt that will wear forever. And looks it. I am planning to wear the coat I find forever, but I don't want to declare the fact; when you are
strapped is the time you never want it to show.

I'll see that it has some kind of collar. The severity of a
cardigan neckline can be ameliorated in a dress or suit by a
scarf or pearls, but I couldn't see myself braving a snow-
storm with a pearl choker around my neck. A coat with its

own scarf is a possibility, but it would be hot on warmer days, and a scarf hanging limply down the front of a coat has a dejected air.

I'd look for a gently fitted coat with an A-line skirt, a modified coachman, or one with a princess line, as long as the waistline didn't hit where a princess's waistline hits, but mine no longer does. Double-breasted would be fine, as my bosom is not magnificent. If it were, the double row of buttons would look as if they were attached to an oversize pincushion. I'd give all buttons a long look. If they were of brass, or had a military air, I'd change them. If I were a small woman, they would make me look like the Little Corporal; as I'm big, like the Ruler of the Queen's Navee. Chances are I'd change the buttons anyway: coat manufacturers, no matter what price range their coats are in, save on buttons, so to replace their buttons with better ones is to add style to any coat. (Practical note: remember to buy at least two more buttons than the number your coat requires, so you won't have to replace the whole regiment if you lose one. And get a tailor to sew them on for you, unless you know his trade secret of how to fix them so they don't fall off the next day.) I'd remove any buttons that had no functional purpose, any belts across the back of the coat, too—they'd only emphasize my hip width.

I've written so much about buttons so far that you may wonder why I don't call the entire clothes section "Button, Button, Who's Got the Button?" To justify the space they occupy forces me to get stuffy, if truthful. The best rule for dressing is to take infinite pains over every detail. Once you've done this, you can then forget the details—forget *ev-*

erything about your clothes—which is the glorious finale you achieve by taking the infinite pains.

If I were small, I'd be particular about pockets, how big they are, where they are placed. Too often I've seen small women with coat pockets that hit their knees: a silly sight.

I wouldn't even bother to look at the coats with fur trim. Fur, if it is any good, adds a whopping amount to the price of a coat. If it's rabbit, who wants it? And gray squirrel is too mousy even to talk about. If I really had my heart set on fur, I'd look for collars, cuffs too, in short-haired furs—beaver, astrakhan, mink, sable. Long-haired furs look busy, so no lynx, which usually appears on shawl collars that are too heavy for an older face to combat, silver fox, which is too reminiscent, anyway, of the thirties, or red fox, too plain vicious to aging skin tones. Fur bands around the hem? Unless you're a Russian dancer, why?

A fur coat wouldn't tempt me. Which is fortunate. Furs have lost their place in high society lately. Preservers of wild life are responsible in part: they have made us, me anyway, squeamish about wearing dead animals. The fashion pacesetters have even rejected Valentina's famous edict "Mink is for football games," or they hide their furs in the linings of cloth coats. (The ultimate put-down was a raincoat lined with mink I saw at a resale shop.) If I still lived in Buffalo, a fur coat might be a temptation, for Nome may be colder than Buffalo, but I have no plans to mush up there to find out.

If I already owned a fur coat, I'd keep it for New York snowstorms—as the blood grows cooler, a very warm coat is a comforting thing—or I'd have it cut down to a jacket, for a fur jacket is fine to have in a climate that presents you with a spring and a fall. I'd wear it over a suit or a two-piece dress if it was not so short that it hit above the jacket. It would certainly be finer than a fur stole: *anything* is better than one of those fitted stoles. A straight stole is possible, if you can drape it over your shoulders with the bravura of a Lauren Bacall. As for those fur pieces of little animals biting each other's tails, they are called tippets, and I'd put them entirely out of my mind.

I'll forget fake furs, furs dyed in wild colors, too, and shaggy mountain-goat or pony tents. It takes youth to carry them off, youth or a devil-may-care stance. I'm aiming for the sterling-silver look; if I can't have the real thing, I'll do without.

Living an urban life necessitates a dressed-up coat for in-between seasons. I'd look for a coat that fits the same requirements I'd ask of a winter dressed-up coat, only in a lighter-weight material. The choice in colors remains constant. Today the seasons flow into each other. It's been a coon's age since navy wasn't seen until after Easter. If I found a coat in navy, I'd never wear it after its lining turned purple, or sadder still, after its shoulders turned rusty from the sun. I wouldn't even consider a short cloth coat—a sixties cliché to be avoided.

I already have a warm coat to wear when I walk Peakie: a fleece-lined storm coat—what we called a General Rommel coat back in the forties—which, in the city or country, is just as right for the seventies. It's right because it is functional, and you know how handsome as well as dateless functional things are. Think on the satisfying design of an eggbeater. The only change thirty years has brought is that

I no longer use the belt, as I've lost my General Rommel waistline. If I did need a casual coat, I would have avoided the car coat, for that would be trespassing on Youth Territory.

There are leather coats to be considered, but not by me in my sixties. The shiny leather coats are out: I'm no retired Easy Rider. The suedes are beautiful but as expensive to keep up as a yacht, for a dirty suede coat is unthinkable. So is a polo coat, for another reason—practically a uniform in the thirties and forties, it would make me look as if I were on a quest for my lost youth if I were to wear one now.

I'm glad now that I bought the London Fog raincoat. It can double as a casual coat. Glad I resisted buying the raincoat that tried with floral patterns to pretend it wasn't a raincoat, for this is as hopeless as the coat you buy to go with everything: it ends up going with nothing, as you know if you've ever seen a short tweed coat worn over an evening dress. Glad, too, I resisted the raincoat with the military air; a secret agent I am not—which is a good reason not to turn up any collar in the back, a raffish touch that's absurdly out of place when it frames a face in its sixties.

I could be tempted by a cape, which has a gothic, romantic look. I'm tall enough to wear one, while a short woman in a cape looks like a mushroom walking. But a friend's admonition would stay my hand: when told I was working on a book, he begged, "Don't be a lady author with three names and a cape." There's a practical deterrent, too. Capes don't offer you any real protection from the wind and the rain.

I won't worry about an evening coat. Not now. I'll substitute a jersey stole for a coat and freeze to death. But I will dream of the perfect evening coat, of tweed, full length, in a rich plum. Or white. A lovely dream.

I won't be conned into buying a costume—a dress with its matching coat—by the argument that I can wear the coat with other dresses. I couldn't. The coat is often lined with the same material the dress is made of, which makes it impossible to wear over any other dress, and it is usually without fastenings or is of three-quarter length, an impossible length to wear with any dress but its own. And the manufacturers waste no time on the dress it accompanies: a tiresome little nothing—and sleeveless.

If I needed any proof that the years had leaped by like a herd of crazy kangaroos, it would be the paucity of notes I had made about suits. For when I was young, suits played a major role in my clothes picture. In those days, they were divided into two types: man-tailored—the severe, broad-lapelled, padded-shoulder suits that Rosalind Russell wore as she sat behind eighteen phones at her lady executive desk—and dressmaker suits—the softer ones, usually sporting a peplum above a very full skirt, that Barbara Stanwyck wore as the salesgirl turned millionaire's wife. I wore neither, I'm proud to say, but I did have tweed suits. They were handsome suits, woven in Scotland, tailored in London, that made me feel I was a handsome girl standing by the bonnie, bonnie banks of Loch Lomond, with a sprig of white heather in my hand and a highland wind in my hair.

But the widening of the hips and the need for softer, kinder lines caused suits to fade in importance, fade and disappear. I expect if I lived in the suburbs I'd still find them an integral part of my clothes life. I see women in them, meeting the 6:04 in Westport; they look neat, but not gaudy.

When they make the mistake of wearing a hat in a matching tweed, however, they look as if they're in uniform. If I wore a suit now, I'd look like Margaret Rutherford, a great way to look if I could find a producer who would cast me in an American version of Miss Marple. But a suit at sixty-seven is a challenge I'm too tired to face.

I may face the challenge of a pantsuit. On other women I see on the street they look comfortable, though I wonder how, if they have looked at their back view, they have found the nerve to buy them. If these women also wear their hair teased and lacquered, I don't wonder why so many of them look a little defiant when they wear pantsuits. They should look not defiant but embarrassed, because they look absurd. Pantsuits require consistency, a casual manner in hairdos and makeup and accessories as well.

If I do succumb to a pantsuit, I'll be sure to have a jacket or a top that is on the loose side and that covers my thighs. I'll see to it that the pants fit properly—no baggy-drawers look from the back, no good-as-exposed crotch in the front—and I won't forget to wear my pantie girdle. I'll never wear high heels with the pantsuit unless it is designed for evening or at home. I'll be sure that the bottoms of the pants are long enough to meet my ankles. And I'll never act as if I wore pants—straddle chairs, sit with my legs apart. I'll continue to act as if I were in a dress.

Come to think about it, I'll continue to wear dresses in town, keep the freedom of a pantsuit for the carefree mood of country living. For while I'm happy to acknowledge that pantsuits are comfortable, I've also realized that the only woman in her sixties whom they flatter is Katharine Hepburn.

VIII

Free and Easy

❧⊰§⊱❧

The young have liberated all of us. Clothes are no longer status symbols. If you live, as I do, in Greenwich Village, you've long ago given up not only trying to figure, as you walk behind a character on its streets, is it a boy or a girl? but also, is he a prince or a pauper? after the first time you see a young man in torn Levi's, ragged tie-dye shirt, and broken sandals slide into the driver's seat of a scarlet Masarati and roar off.

It's one world for the young—one free world. In fashions, the world is theirs, and everything that's in it. Free as the wind, they circle the globe, picking up a sari from India, a burnous from Algeria, a beaded headband from New Mexico. Today they can be a proud African queen in a caftan, tomorrow a gypsy fortune-teller in ruffled skirts and chains of beads. Conformity is as dead as the bobby sock.

It's great, this new freedom, and refreshing. And like any form of freedom, it brings along its own responsibility: the responsibility of choice. Not for the young, but for those who are in the sixties. Casual clothes, the trade's name for what you wear in your relaxed hours, have always been freer than any others. Now, with the world to choose from, a careful choice becomes more necessary than ever to us. You don't have to be an isolationist in fashion, but you do have to be wary of foreign entanglements if you want to feel at ease. Granted that today in a big city you could walk down the street in a nightgown without anyone making a citizen's arrest for indecent exposure, but would you feel at ease?

Of course, if you are somebody who has long since established herself as a character, you will throw this book across the room and go right on wearing your broad-brimmed black sombrero. Great! It's Power to the Eccentrics! every time. But if you are not that self-confident or, like Beau Brummel, feel that if people stare at you, you are not well-dressed, you'll evaluate an ethnic fashion in terms of your present age before you succumb to a sarape.

I've invented a practical trick to keep myself from disastrous choices: I slip the word *old* in front of the description of an ethnic or historical style. If tempted by a fringed cowgirl shirt, I have only to say "an *old* cowgirl?" to cool my ardor. An elaborate Japanese kimono: "an *old* geisha girl?" A multipocketed canvas coat: "an *old* white hunter?" It works every time.

Your own home is where you too can be free as the wind.

You can make it your pagoda, your seraglio, your Casbah, your Shangri-la. Pick your country when you pick your robe or housecoat. Lightweight wools, velvets in brilliant colors, even ruffles, provided they become you, printed silks that are like gardens of flowers—they are all yours for the wearing at home. There are limits: unless you're Mae West, chances are you'll feel pretty silly in satins and marabou.

Let your choice be a long robe, for a long robe will make you feel you're quite a person, and that's a lovely way to feel when your family comes, or your friends. And when you are alone. Especially when you are alone, for then you need the assurance, more then than at any other time, that you are quite a person. Slopping around by yourself in your oldest dress won't do it. Thank the Lord I don't have to say, "Or in a housedress." *They've* gone with the wind and the boudoir cap, and good riddance to both of them.

You will need another housecoat or bathrobe to put on in the morning when it's too early to be a maharani and you have to answer, with thumping heart, the doorbell. You'd do well to greet the mugger who turns out to be the mailman in a washable one. Washable so you will always look spanking clean: an even slightly dirty housecoat can turn the most respectable woman into a slattern.

Not slatternly but feminine as all get-out is a frilly bed jacket, a fine thing to have around, not only when you're laid low with a cold, but for when you want to read in bed or imitate the queens in the old days and hold court in your bedroom. Avoid ecru lace—too brownish for you—or peek-aboo eyelet cottons—unfortunately, you are past inciting anybody's urge to peek. Also to be ignored are knitted wool bed jackets, for a reason at the other end of the scale: they'll turn you into Little Red Riding Hood's grandmother.

In clothes for the country you can let yourself go, but now that you are sixty, the question arises how far? The young have made Levi's the uniform of their international brigade. Won't you feel foolish as an overage recruit if you wear them? Keep a pair in your closet, though, for when you have to clean out the cistern.

You can't avoid slacks. Look for well-proportioned ones, with straight pant legs. (Bell-bottoms? Don't be absurd!) They offer warmth in the winter, freedom of movement any time of the year. You can plant a tulip, climb a mountain, sail a boat, and never fret that somebody is going to tell *you* to pull down your skirt. I'd be the last one to suggest you give them up. They can be, if not flattering to you, acceptable to your public if you choose, with the acumen of a marriage broker, what you team them up with. The kind of material in the shirt you wear with them doesn't matter. The type of shirt doesn't matter, so long as you can wear it over your slacks, not tucked in. *That* matters. There are few of us in our sixties who want to emphasize our waistline, many of us who want to hide our hipline. With shirts we can go international ourselves—wear porters' smocks from Germany, fishermen's shirts from Brittany, wedding shirts from Mexico or Greece. Avoid the conventional smock, unless you work in a beauty parlor, and smocked or yoked shirts; they emphasize the falling, if not fallen, breast line. But then, you wouldn't be attracted to them, anyway, as you doubtless have bidden the winsome and the coy look good-bye, along with dirndls and pinafores. I hope you haven't said good-bye to jumpers. Those with a tailored bent, worn with a casual shirt in the daytime or with an elegant long-sleeved one at night, are great flatterers.

And you'll never, if you're wise, give up the crisp and shiny look of an apple. The fresh look of youth can overcome sloppiness in young people, but there's nothing to justify it when you're older. Crisp, translated, means everything we wear is right off a clothesline that is stretched across a yard bright with sunlight and warm winds, or looks that way if we choose clean fabrics like chambrays, seersuckers, and denims. Denims forever!

Matching slipovers and cardigans that pick up the colors of a tweed skirt are country and suburban banalities. They are a safe fashion, and a dull one. Safe or not, they are less flattering than a dress and a sweater. (I'm not talking about the print dress with its cardigan decorated around the neckline with flowers of the same material. *That* is the queen of all banalities.)

No sweater should be of heavy wool or weave, which will weigh you down if you're thin and add to your massive look if you're fat. This rules out the handsome Irish ones. A turtleneck sweater will hide your aging neck, but unless you pull it up to your widow's peak, it can't obliterate the fact that you are a little too long in the tooth to be coxswain in the Oxford shell.

A white sweater is a go-with-everything convenience. It is also a cliché of the sixties. It is a grandmother sweater—today's version of grandma's shawl. A cardigan jacket of flannel or any lightweight wool or a Chanel-type jacket carries more style with it, as does a blazer, if it doesn't sport an emblazoned insignia on its breast pocket. My "old" ploy works here: who at sixty wants to be an *old* Eton boy? This also rules out knickers: an *old* Blue Boy?

A danger inherent in many country clothes is their tendency to make the wearer look masculine. When it's practical and necessary, because it's cold, to wear lumberjack tops or windbreakers, subdue their masculine look with a pretty scarf or a pair of earrings, because the softness of femininity is our dish of tea. Defy Rudi Gernreich's prophecy that soon all clothes will be bisexual.

Men are luckier than women in casual clothes: they know how to look cool and/or relaxed without looking sloppy. Though they can make mistaken choices, too. I have always admired Harry Truman for his spunk, but I have never forgiven him his tacky sport shirts, noisy with printed palm fronds. And a man with the top of his head as bald as a knob on a brass bed, whose hair flows over the back of his turtleneck sweater atop his bell-bottomed slacks, is about as absurd-looking as a sixty-year-old man can get.

Summer is a dangerous time. When it's hot you'll be tempted to wear shorts. Don't. Unless if you live on a remote island on the equator where the mail boat comes over the horizon only once a year, perhaps a pair of bermuda shorts. Otherwise, forget them. Forever. Next to the wrong hat, but nudging it for first place, shorts are the cruelest thing any older woman can do to herself. Way back there when I was young, playsuits were the thing, one-piece affairs of a top and shorts with a matching skirt. They were a fine idea. They still are, if you can sew. You won't find them around in shops anymore. If you can't, be of good cheer—a crisp cotton dress is almost as cool as shorts, and think of the disaster, the look of you in shorts, it will have averted.

I'm sure it's not necessary to mention the impossibility of tank-suit tops. Halter neckline. Stretch pants. One-piece jump suits. Or, on the beach, two-piece, bikini bathing suits. It's the soft, draped bathing suit for you, with as long an overskirt as you can find, and with a terry cape to cover you up when you're not swimming. You weren't born yesterday. *You* know it, but do you want to spell it out in neon lights?

IX

Accessories to the Crime

❧⟨⟩☙

When I used to put on fashion shows back in the forties, when I was forty, I was often given a hard time by the models. They weren't professional models, but members of whatever women's club was sponsoring the show. It was a breeze to dress the younger models: confident in their youth, they would wear anything. The better-heeled the model, too, the more relaxed she would be about what she was asked to wear because, sad to relate, her money gave her the security not to give a damn.

My store put on these fashion shows to create goodwill. I would not be creating goodwill if I cracked the whip over the models, so the fittings were as tense as a U.N. debate. The accessories triggered the tensest moments. The older members were conservative about accessories, remembering such outdated adages as "Black goes with everything" and "All accessories must be the same color." There were never many younger people around to persuade them otherwise. Often enough there was a minority of one young model—a daughter bludgeoned into service to wear the bride's dress. The clubs always demanded a bridal party as the finale of the fashion show. I never could figure out why, though, since the members' wedding dresses had long ago turned yellow in their tissue-paper nests. Maybe they wanted to cry a little over the dreams of glory they had dreamed when they were brides?

These hassles over accessories were such frustrating experiences for me that I figured out an antidote. I evolved a mini-fashion show that was offered to clubs as a luncheon feature, an accessories version of the before-and-after approach used in advertising. I called the peripatetic show "Striptease." If you find that arch, you're right, but you also don't remember the forties. That title was then as daring as Ernest Hemingway's substitution of the word *obscenity* for what were then considered obscene words. Today I'd call my show "Accessories to the Crime," which is equally arch. And equally valid. For, as a valuable old cliché has it, "it's not what you put on, it's what you take off that's important." If there are too many accessories, or if they are too big or too flamboyant, they are then guilty of the crime of busyness.

In the forties, with an over-forty volunteer standing by my side, looking as noisy and crowded as a subway platform at rush hour, wearing a red hat, red earrings, red pin, red handbag, red gloves, and red shoes with a noisy colored dress, I would make my pitch for serenity. I'd open with the question that always startled the audience to attention, "Why do we think all nuns are beautiful?" and answer, "Because their habits don't distract with busy accessories." (Today many orders have given up wearing habits. It must be a relief to the nuns not to be weighted down by heavy, long skirts and long, loose sleeves, but they lost their serenity when they discarded the medieval austerity of their habits.)

I'd then introduce the volunteer, and begin subtracting accessories from her, begin the striptease.

I substituted, never subtracted, her hat. Perhaps in the 1970s nobody but hat manufacturers will agree with me, but I feel it is a crying shame that hats have gone into semi-retirement—except with the young, who have rediscovered their fun and flattery—for if properly chosen, hats top the list of friendly accessories. They are enemies if they are not consistent with your style and your age; they can make you look ridiculous, comic, absurd. An enemy hat is one that is not in proportion to your size and face: a tall hat that fails to add height to a short woman or a hat with a broad brim that makes her look as if she were hiding under an umbrella. On a tall woman, it's a beanie that makes her look like an old-fashioned clothespin. The heavily flowered hat or the hat that isn't a hat but a veil, crowded with bows and fake cherries that bounce, transform any woman into a replica of Helen Hokinson's famous women's club presidents.

All the hats that demand a young face to carry them off are enemies: the schoolboy cap, the stocking cap, jockey cap, newsboy's cap, elf's cap, the tam-o'-shanter (if you want or need to wear a knitted hat in winter, take off its pom-pom), the sou'wester, the baby bonnet tied under the chin, the boater with the little-girl streamers. And as for the big velvet bow worn at the back of the head! Never! Scarves can be cruel if they are tied tight under your chins, or sport jocund designs, like a clown with his performing seal. If draped loosely over your head, they can compliment your face. The cruelest of all headcovers is the Glad bag, or plastic rainhat. The boredom of carrying an umbrella is preferable anytime.

Hostile, too, are hats stolen from men: the derby, top hat, fedora, cowboy hat, the gaucho hat, the sailor. Their hard lines are hard on you, unless you want to look like a man. If you do, it's unlikely you'll be reading this book.

There's an irony about hats: the most beautiful ones are designed for young faces, but only rich older women can afford them. But there are friendly hats to be found at hat bars if you're not rich. Friendly because they are becoming frames that can soften the square jaw, minimize the double chin, emphasize the eyes.

In the accessory playlet, I'd remove from the volunteer's head the hat whose crown looked like an inverted pot-de-chambre, and replace it with a big-brimmed hat—if she were tall enough to carry it off—or a soft-draped turban, one of the most flattering of hats. I'd see that she left enough of her hair showing, for unless a face has the perfect symmetry of a Dolores Del Rio, a turban can be too demanding. Or give her a beret, a generously sized beret. (The true beret, the French one, is too small for most older faces, or gives them the look of professional liberals.) Or a fez. Or a pillbox. Again, one in proportion to her face, the key phrase for hats. Or I'd give her the friendliest of hats for all faces—

thin, fat, long, or round—the hat with the rolled brim. I'd emphasize, too, where the volunteer put the hat on her head. Wearing it straight and low on the forehead is a dirty trick to play on any face; tipping it to one side creates a rakish look—only good if you're still a rake. Wearing it on the back of your head gives your hair the chance to fulfill its obligation to be a kind frame to your face.

After cleaning up the hat situation, I'd go to work on the jewelry. I'd start by taking off the earrings that matched or picked up the color of the volunteer's dress and substituting pearl or gold or silver ones in designs whose lines went up to balance the lines of an older face that were going down. I'd never let her wear hanging earrings for the same reason. And because they are noisy. That reason would call for the removal of most of her bracelets as well, or at least any that jangled, jangled. *Ankle* bracelets? Please. Plastic? Plastic jewelry, like plastic anything, becomes the young only, because, like plastic, youth is temporary. Age is here to stay.

Next I'd remove the pin the volunteer wore (or if I left it on, I would subtract another piece of jewelry in its place), especially if it was a round circle pin—the insignia of the Ivy League college girl. The "amusing" pin, too, for the poodle with the rhinestone beard and the owl with the emerald eye are cute, and who, at sixty, wants to be cute? (Exception: if it's a present from a grandson it will be cherished, but kept to wear when his grandmother takes him to lunch.) If you're lucky enough to have a diamond pin, or one with real stones, you'll want to subtract some other accessory to wear it.

But think twice before you subtract a pearl necklace. Carol Channing may sing that diamonds are a girl's best friend, but when you're over fifty, pearls are yours. Antediluvian is the rule that a lady's pearls must be real, but they should be clean, which calls for frequent washings, and artificial ones thrown away when they turn yellow. A two-strand pearl choker is your best bet, if not worn high enough to choke. Long strands of pearls are currently popular, but for you in your sixties, shorter lengths are more discreet. Long strands, if you're flat-chested, emphasize your flatness; if big-bosomed, bounce between Scylla and Charybdis.

If you have collected jewelry from other times or other places, be sure it is not too heavy or too distracting or too far-out. My mother wore with innocent pride a silver Indian necklace from Santa Fe, until my gentle father felt obligated to tell her that by the shape of its pendant, it was obviously designed as a fertility symbol.

A couplet that has now lost its validity is "Men seldom make passes/At girls who wear glasses." The young have made them legitimate. If you're no longer young, it would be sensible to avoid the outsize types, the Ben Franklin's, the harlequins, the granny glasses that are not flattering to grannies. Avoid that chain to hold them around your neck, too: convenient at times, but so trite in the sixties. And keep your dark glasses for the sunny days alone. They hide what is usually your best feature, your eyes, to bring into prominence what is often your worst, your mouth. For in the sixties, if your eyes are the windows of your soul, your mouth is the narrator of your life, and too often your life is reflected in narrowing lips or lips that curve downward. If you have to wear glasses all the time, count them as an accessory, which means you should subtract some other accessory from your total look to make room for them.

Scarves are great—long may they wave! For the sixties especially, they are staunch allies. If they are properly trained, if they are arranged in the neckline of your dress or suit so that they stay put there. It's a good idea to pin them the way you want them in order to spare your audience the disconcerting sight of you fumbling with them as you're tempted to do if you don't pin them down. Unpinned, they invite fussy attention on the order of other such nervous-making moves as clutching young people as you talk to them, pulling down your girdle, rearranging the bosoms in your bra, and diving into your dress to adjust your slip straps.

Scarves present an easy way of bringing white close to your face, if pearls give you claustrophobia. If you choose a white scarf, let it be one that boasts a pattern in another color: an all-white scarf can too easily be mistaken for a bandage. Eschew large scarves if your neck is on the short side, or the scarf tied ascot fashion, unless you plan to ride to hounds.

Never does size—your size—dictate more pragmatically than when you choose the size of your pocketbook: a small woman can, by carrying a big bag, transform herself into a porter; a big woman with a small bag can look as if she's stolen her granddaughter's play purse. Any bag is a better investment, in economy as well as style, if it is in real leather. (Practical note: keep a can of saddle soap in your closet and polish your bag; it's good for your shoes, too. And have a brush on hand for suede.) Bags with a shoulder strap are convenient but dangerously youth-oriented. At the other extreme, hanging a bag by its straps over your forearm adds years to your appearance, as I wish somebody would point out to Queen Elizabeth.

In those fashion talks I always had to force myself to talk about *shoes*. I would tend to forget them because I have very big feet and grew up in an era when ladies were expected to have small feet like little mice peering from under their skirts. (Greta Garbo's big feet freed women of that tradition.) So I always looked for, and had a terrible time finding, the plainest pumps—I had to fight my way through fields of orthopedic oxfords. Now it's accepted that lots of girls have big feet, so it's possible to find pretty shoes in all sizes. Be wary of that prettiness, though. Here again, the recognition of your age affects your choice—Mary Janes and pert, Debbie Reynolds bows on pumps are not for you. Neither are ballet slippers, except with your long robe at home.

Open toes, harlequin combinations of colors, shiny leathers are all OK for the occasional Highland Fling, but the pump is still the most becoming and the most comfortable, if the heels are not too high. We have a tendency to totter a bit in the sixties, anyway, and very high heels force us to take the short steps of a mechanical doll who has just been wound up with a giant key. In the country, as well as at home, there is more freedom to wear espadrilles, huaraches, and tennis shoes, as well as ballet slippers. (Practical note: go shopping for shoes after a long walk, or on a hot day. If they feel comfortable then, they'll have you walking on clouds when you get them home. Unless they're patent leather. It yields to nothing.)

If you think I've left out one type of shoe—sandals—you're right. And for the best of reasons: feet aren't the prettiest part of our anatomy at any age, except perhaps when we are babies. I found that out the night before I got married. My mother said, "Lavinia, I want to talk to you. Alone." I, at twenty-one, feeling so sophisticated (I *had* just read Havelock Ellis), whined, as she dragged me into the hotel bathroom and shut the door, "Oh, *Mother*. Please. I know all about the birds and bees!" "Never mind about the birds and bees," Mother said. "Just remember this. You and your sister have the ugliest toenails west of the Mississippi. So always cover them with colored nail polish." So I always did, until the last ten years when, like strong-colored nail polish on my fingernails, it only directed attention, so I've retired my feet. I cover them up with shoes, or wear stockings.

Stockings took no time to be discussed in the forties. How exciting they've become since—pantie hose in wild colors and wild patterns. Sorry—not at sixty. We've been liberated—we don't have to worry anymore if our seams are straight—but we had better leave the wild patterns to the young. And the wild colors. As well as black and white. *If* we don't want to invite the reaction "Why, she's sixty if she's a day." For the lovely thing that happens when you dress your age is that nobody thinks about your age. While if you wear young fashions, you force your audience to become conscious of your age—and start them speculating on the exact number of years you've tallied up.

Boots have now come into fashion view: choose them with care. In black or brown, they are warm and practical. Hip-length, in shiny leather, in white or crazy colors, laced through brass hooks, they promise a youthful appearance to the young man following you on the street, a disappointment when he catches up with you.

Gloves didn't take up much time then, nor would they now. Like hats, they are no longer obligatory except for church, weddings, receptions, and grand-gala bashes. Unless you are like a dear friend of mine, a born-and-bred New Yorker, who when she once saw me rushing out without any gloves on, said, "I'd rather walk down Fifth Avenue in my bare feet than go without gloves." You will avoid as much as you would wearing hair curlers outside your house fancy gloves—the net or lace or the heavily embroidered variety—as well as the short, short glove you wore once to dancing school. With a couple of pairs of plain, hand-stitched fabric gloves in a neutral shade (white gloves *don't* go with everything) and one pair of long chamois gloves for the elegant moments, you're all set. If you live in a cold climate, however, you'll want warm wool-lined or knitted gloves—but never baby mittens—for winter.

Let flowers, if you wear them, be real flowers, for there are adjectives you never want your appearance to invite. Dusty is one, artificial is another. By your age, you have earned the real thing. I created a pleasing effect once by tucking a real, almost full-blown rose into the ribbon on a big navy milan hat that I wore with a navy chiffon shirtdress to a garden wedding. If you have to wear a corsage, and the times turn up when you do have to wear one, if you don't want to be boorish to the kind people who sent it to you, take off all the goo—the ferns, the ribbons—from it. Never wear a corsage pinned to your shoulder. Tuck it in your waist—if you still have a waist—or in the V of your dress, if your dress has a V neckline. A pink or red camellia tucked into the V of a chiffon dress can be a pretty grace note. And it won't turn brown like a gardenia. (Reminder: be sure to count flowers as another accessory, when you're doing your style arithmetic.) If you have neither waistline nor V neck, Scotch-tape the corsage on your evening bag. Yes, that's tacky too, but you can always put your bag down somewhere.

I always wanted to put on a flower fashion show (Allied Florists, please note, I'm still available) and use them as the chief accessory. It would be great fun to figure out which flowers brighten which dress, coat, or suit. A couple of daisies tucked into the buttonhole of an Irish tweed coatdress, a bold orange dahlia on the lapel of a black and white tweed coat, a couple of purple anemones pinned on the collar of a swinging navy cape, a small spray of yellow butterfly orchids over a chignon, a circlet of daisies and bachelor buttons for bridesmaids. (Not for bridesmaids over sixty! Or anybody over sixty!) Clare Boothe Luce always wore one perfect rose when she was a congresswoman; Senator Margaret Chase Smith has carried on with the tradition, a feminine and a pretty conceit. It must, of course, be fresh as well as perfect.

One of the pleasant freedoms imagination gives is to experiment, to improvise, to take something out of its usual place and adapt it to a new use. One of the freshest wedding bouquets I ever saw—it was for a second wedding—was a corsage of white geraniums arranged in a flattened-down bunch, circled with green and white ivy. On the bride's dove gray wool dress, it struck an elegant note.

I always ended the accessory show by pinning a flower

on the lapel of the volunteer's shirtdress. She would stand there, no longer a busy Christmas tree, but a triumph of serenity, which brought her a round of applause from the club members. I have no way of knowing how many women are now walking around triumphs of serenity because of her, but I do know that no matter what tornadoes are raging inside of me, now on the outside I look as tranquil as a morning in May.

X

You Don't Have
to Break Your Hip

❧❦❧

"Avoid fried foods which anger the blood. If your stomach disputes you, lie down and pacify it with cooling thoughts. Keep your juices flowing by jangling around gently as you move. Go very lightly on the vices such as carrying on in society—the social ramble ain't restful. Avoid running at all times." Those are the rules that Satchel Paige, an old baseball player, laid down for a healthy life, and I plan to follow them to the letter. I'll add a few of my own that I've discovered on my way to the sixties.

I'm not only going to avoid fried food, I'm going to go easy on eating generally. No baseball player, I don't need the heavy shipments of fuel that food supplies. I've found I do have more energy if I have five small meals a day rather than three big ones. I'll emulate the British: they know the wisdom of the pauses that refresh with their elevenses and their teatimes. Having fought weight all my life, I can count calories in my sleep, so it's no problem to divide their total by five and thus not add more pounds. The number of meals used to be six until I woke up to the fact that what I ate just before I went to bed turned into pounds before I went to sleep, and the pounds stayed with me unless I exiled them with still another diet. I've learned not to experiment with diets. My body is no longer resilient enough to take the violent ups and downs of crash diets without paying me back with fatigue or depression or both. The next time my appetite has overcome my vanity, I won't experiment with the newest diet. I'll go to a doctor for a road map.

I won't use eating as a way to pass the time. Food can become a time killer when you're older, if there is a paucity of other occupations. All you have to do is watch the older guests at a resort for verification. They gather in the lobby waiting for the dining-room doors to open, so eager are they to indulge their last passion. Their deliberation as they choose which vegetable to have becomes as grave a decision as a president's choice of cabinet members.

If I were a good cook, I could derive pleasure in whipping up dishes to delight friends and family, but I never mastered the art. So I'll dust the stove and take my friends out to dinner. And live on hamburgers and chef's salad when I'm by myself. I will be careful not to go to the other extreme and live on mouse food. Too often for comfort, solitude kills the appetite. Women alone forget to eat, or to eat properly, then wonder why they feel lassitude and depression when they have laid themselves open to anemia.

I'll subdivide my amount of sleep, too. I won't need as much of it as when I was more active, but I'll be more refreshed by it if I have it more often. Older people, like babies, have a way of waking up early in the morning, and, like babies, their early waking can be a pain in the neck to those around them. The older people don't demand a bottle, but they can demand coffee, or wake up the entire house by rattling around the kitchen at an uncivilized hour while they make it themselves. (Practical note: a thermos of coffee, cadged the night before, will obviate that antisocial caper.)

But early to bed and early to rise means you're suddenly very sleepy at very odd times. A nap before lunch, after lunch, before or after teatime, any time that fits into your schedule is the delicious answer. The going-to-sleep part of it is delicious; the waking up can be dismal. Get up quickly, wash your face, drink a cup of something, or take your dog for a fast walk. Take your catnaps in the solitude of your room. Babies asleep are beautiful. As you grow older, and older, sleep brings with it snores, gaping mouth, and drooling out of one side of it. You are not beautiful.

You can be a bore if you insist on reporting your nightly sleep record. Nobody finds it stop-the-press news if you slept only two hours. Nobody believes it when you report you never slept a wink last night. At your age, you're expected to be smart enough to do something about it, to turn on the light and finish your mystery in the middle of the night, to take a nap during the day, or go to bed earlier the next night.

You don't have to sleep to rest. It's a grand idea to lie down every chance you can devise. It's more comfortable to lie down than to sit down, more reviving to sit down than to stand up. Take the most comfortable chair when it's offered. Don't hesitate, if one is around, to head direct for the rocking chair. President Kennedy broke down the old tradition that the comfort of a rocking chair belongs only to the old. Resist the low chair. It is as awkward to get out of as a car, now that running boards are anachronisms.

Comfort is becoming, because it is an admission that you have accepted age and its fringe benefits. You *are* getting older. The steps aren't getting steeper. You don't have to prove you're just as good as you ever were. Many a poor soul is dead because he tried to prove it by shoveling the snow off his driveway. If, like Robert Benchley, you've always felt that exercise is a form of nervous disorder, you won't feel guilty if you don't play touch football with your grandchildren, but you may call yourself a lazy slob if you avoid all exercise. I've bought enough gadgets—rollers, stationary bicycles, ropes—to open a gymnasium. They are gathering dust balls in my closet. I've settled for croquet and walks with Peakie. If I had been athletic, I would want to continue at a more leisurely pace the sport I enjoyed. If it were sanctioned by my doctor.

I plan to check all my physical plans with a doctor. For, unless you are a Christian Scientist, a doctor is now the most valuable man or woman in your life. You won't make a move without his consent. You won't launch yourself on new seas—on yogurt or yoga, on new vitamins, pharmaceutical or natural, on the newest form of jigging or jogging—without checking in with him first. If you already have a family doctor, you are in luck. He has been the coauthor of your body's biography, so he can help you block out the next chapters in a matter of moments. With a new doctor it will take a little longer, but a complete physical will tell him all he needs to know. A yearly checkup is a sound idea after sixty, as is a check on your glasses. Many an older woman goes around convinced her sight is failing, when all she needs is stronger lenses.

A doctor can be your father confessor. In his office you can feel free to bring out into the open day all the doubts and fears that have tormented you in the dark of the night. It is inevitable that you can't live sixty years without your body springing a leak somewhere. If he is an understanding doctor, he'll not laugh off your pain but reassure you by identifying it as one of the occupational hazards of the sixties, will tell you that you're stuck with it, perhaps prescribe a pill to minimize the discomfort.

I'll look for a doctor who will give me a pill. Being no stoic, I'll take any pill that a doctor will give me, to alleviate pain, to help me sleep, to increase energy. I'll stick with the dentist, too, who gives me a shot of Novocaine before he touches a tooth. I don't feel I'm letting down our side by benefiting from all that the research scientists and doctors have been at in laboratories.

I won't abuse a doctor's compassion by trying to use him as an antidote to boredom or loneliness. That cautionary note went into my notebook when I lived in La Jolla, a lovely haven for older people who are well-fixed, where there are as many doctors' offices on the main street as shops. It was there that I heard blue-haired ladies greet each other of a morning not with the conventional "Hello, how are you?" but with "Well, what did he say about you today?" Down in the notebook, too, went the pathetic wail of a lonely woman in a big city: "All the doctors nowadays are so young, they won't take the time to listen to me."

I won't expect a doctor to give me a happiness pill. Edith Wharton said: "There are lots of ways of being miserable, but there's only one way of being comfortable. And that is to stop running around after happiness. If you make up your mind not to be happy, there is no reason why you shouldn't have a fairly good time." I shall expect a doctor to help me be comfortable by helping me devise a master plan for a health regime. I'll adjust my habits to his suggestions. With his advice, I'll accept age. I won't accept as inevitable that I shall break my hip, a sixty-up catastrophe that often occurs in the bathroom. But I'll get one of those gadgets to hold on to when I get out of the tub, to prevent it, if possible. If I do grow lame, I'll find the handsomest ebony cane available and use it with style. If I grow deaf, I'll admit it by using a hearing aid.

I won't use pills to escape from the life I'm stuck with. If it's so unpalatable, I'll go about changing it. Neither will I use liquor as a glass crutch. Long before women were allowed in bars, and before alcoholism was admitted out loud as a social problem, lonely, unhappy women were nipping away in the privacy of their bedrooms. When their steps grew unsteady, their words blurred, the reason given was that "Mother's had a little too much of her tonic." Many of the tonics were 90 percent alcohol.

Sometimes, as you grow older, something strange happens to your metabolism, when it comes to the consumption of liquor. My father used to take a highball every night before he went to bed. He said, "Whiskey is an old man's milk." Its only effect on him was to send him to sleep quickly. It's been a different story with me. I used to take great delight in drinking. I could put away vats of it without going to rack and to ruin. I was always proud of the compliment my stepson gave me: that in drinking I had a wooden leg. I relished the shift in values liquor accomplished: all the serious things—money, health, survival—became trivial, and all the lighter things, the absurd remark, the unexpected smile, the hilarious hat, became important. But with increasing years, I found one drink would depress me, would threaten me with a crying jag. I checked with a doctor to discover why, and he told me it was due to a shift in my metabolism. I stopped drinking. If it no longer guaranteed fun, why bother with it? Abstinence won't turn me into a belligerent Carrie Nation, won't keep me from having liquor at home for those who do drink or cigarettes for smokers. Trying to reform other people's habits is worse than presumptuous. It is damned bad manners.

I checked with the doctor, too, about smoking. He didn't recommend it as a habit, but, as of the last checkup, found no bad effects from it. When or if he does, I'll stop that habit, too. I'll continue not to smoke in bed. Always a risky habit, it becomes downright dangerous when you are older and sleep comes without warning.

If I were still married and found myself unhappy in bed, I'd ask the doctor for advice or for the name of a psychiatrist he trusted. If by sixty I hadn't resolved my sex life, I'd need help, but I wouldn't mistake the analyst's couch for a haven from boredom or loneliness.

The rest of my physical life will be my responsibility. For

one thing, I will not indulge myself in sickness. I have always found that a job can get me out of bed, dry up a cold, and cure a headache. But I *will* find out the telephone number of a good visiting-nurse agency, so that if I'm trapped by a bug that isn't bad enough to put me in the hospital but is serious enough to keep me in bed for a considerable time, I can call on them rather than on my busy children to come in and take over.

I will acknowledge to myself that sickness brings the blues along with it. I've come to some pretty dreary conclusions about myself when I was laid low with a cold. They may have been accurate conclusions, but they were also pointless. A mea-culpa session is an exercise in futility that debilitates your spirit. Too often I've lain in bed sniffling and coughing as I watched in my mind reruns of all my old movies. And any plans for the future I ever made while in this low state were inevitably so tinged with the gray of despair that I always had to scrap them when recovery brought courage back to me.

I will accept the necessity to be gentle with myself. In summer, I'll walk on the shady side of the street. When I want to pick up a pin from the floor—I'm always sure I'll never straighten up again, but will fall flat in a Mack Sennett sprawl—I'll kneel before I pick it up. I'll walk, not run, to meet the sunset. I won't leap out of bed: I'll turn slowly on my side and ease out of it. If I have twinges in my left shoulder, I'll look at the moon over my right one.

I'll avoid reading the columns on health in the papers, for I know my inclination to make every symptom described my own. I'll give a quick look at the obituaries, but won't waste time comparing the ages mentioned with my own.

Above all, I won't be ashamed of my age. I'll be proud that, like John Berryman, "I'm still here, severely damaged, but functioning." My pride will show in the way I carry myself. There's something heroic about a straight back. (Practical note: good posture, according to many doctors, can prevent bad backs.) Many older women bend over without any physical reason for doing it, because they feel it's expected of them. I won't walk with my toes pointing outward, like a penguin, won't shift my weight from side to side in the rolling gait of a sailor. I'll slant forward, like young people, when I walk, not lean backward like the old. For like the young, I want to hurry to what's ahead of me. I'll not accept "declining" as the adjective to describe the years ahead of me. I shall, instead, add to the golden number of my years more golden numbers. I shan't retire myself from living.

I shall add one more clause to Satch Paige's philosophy. I shall add gusto. It's a better tonic than Geritol, any day, for "a merry heart doeth good like a medicine: but a broken spirit drieth the bones." It is gusto that keeps Casals playing. A musician in his orchestra told me it was like watching a miracle to see Casals conduct. He almost had to be helped onto the podium, for after all, he is in his nineties, but the minute he started the rehearsal, he shed twenty-five or thirty years. Let's not put it in figures, say rather that he became ageless. That is what gusto can do for *me*. It can help me achieve the goal I'm aiming for—not to feel young for my age, but to have such a rich time living that I don't even think about my age. I plan to enjoy it so much that when I'm ninety I will be able to say, like Justice Holmes, "Oh, to be seventy again!"

XI

Mothers-in-Law Are No Joke

❧⬥❧

I couldn't wait to be a mother-in-law. I'd been lucky in mothers-in-law myself. I had had two and both were great, both stomped to pieces all the old mother-in-law jokes. I'm sure, if given the choice of a daughter-in-law, my first mother-in-law, a devout Irish Catholic whose whole world was her husband and her eight children, would never have picked me. I was a girl who not only was an agnostic, and about as domestic as Elizabeth Taylor, but was determined to live the gypsy life with her youngest son. But when he did choose me, she welcomed me with unquestioning affection. She also made friends with my dog, a remarkable demonstration of devotion from her, because, frightened by all animals, she had never before had a pet in her house.

My second mother-in-law, a gentle lady, badly bruised but not destroyed by tragedy, gave an equally generous welcome to me—a woman who was no longer young, with one marriage that had failed on her record. She underlined her generosity by her loving welcome to my two children. My own mother, in her offbeat, often frustrating way, was also an unusual mother-in-law: she always took the side of her son-in-law.

I was determined to combine the best features of all three when my turn as a mother-in-law came up. When my son brought home a girl, my daughter a boy, or either surprised me with a wife or husband, I hoped I would accept them literally with open arms. If my son loved the girl enough to want her for a wife, my daughter loved the boy enough to risk the perils of marriage, that was all I would need to know to love them, too. I started to draw up the master plan the night I waited up for a daughter to come back from her first dance.

The most important item on my agenda was my resolve to Let Go. The hardest part of letting go is to accept the truth that the words in the marriage service, "I now pronounce you man and wife," automatically reduce you as a mother to the status of a second-rate citizen in your child's world. From that moment on, your son is a husband before he is a son, your daughter is a wife before she is a daughter. If those words don't accomplish those changes, I'd be ashamed of the way I'd raised my children. It would ease me into my role of supporting actor to remember a line said by a new young wife: "I dreamed his mother and I were drowning, and he rescued *me*."

With or without marriage, my children were going to go,

anyway. I wanted the credit from them, as well as for my own pride, to be the first to let go. I'd wave them off with encouraging cries of "Bon voyage!" "Have a fine time!" If it worked out as well with them as it had with me and my parents, they would return to me as friends.

My son- and daughter-in-law would also become my friends if I remembered that all young men and women are conditioned to suspect mothers-in-law, whether consciously or not, by the cartoons and the comedians' tired jokes about them. The mother-in-law stands in a niche next to the step-mother as an established villainess. And with some reason: you don't have to be Jewish to be a Jewish mother or mother-in-law, a woman who by tradition makes a career of making her child feel guilty. If my son forgets to telephone on Mother's Day, I'll thank God that he is so busy being happy with his wife he didn't have the time to remember.

I'd follow the plan by never giving advice, unless I were asked for it. I'd never reach down in my ragbag of maxims to pull out a one-liner like this page-filler from the *Reader's Digest*, "It isn't Life itself that counts, but the courage you put into it." Or a maxim of my own invention, for mother-hood doesn't make me eligible for a seat on Olympus. Motherhood, unless the parent is constantly on the alert, often turns an originally free, happy-go-lucky girl into a walking book of maxims and morals. It results from the ab-surd belief that the act of giving birth transforms a girl into an all-wise Earth Mother, a belief that has turned many a young, exuberant girl into a guilt-ridden old hag.

I'll remember how it feels to be on the receiving end of advice. When I'm low, and somebody says, "You'll feel dif-ferently tomorrow," that somebody is in grave peril of losing her teeth and my friendship. Her advice is often true, but who wants to hear the truth when unhappy? If I am momentarily low, I'll avoid seeing my children until my sun comes out from the clouds, will avoid talking to them by not answering the phone. It took sixty years to learn how to overcome the telephone's tyranny through the simple expedient of not picking up the receiver when it rings, but the resulting freedom has been well worth waiting for.

And who wants to hear she looks bad? "Frankly" or "to tell you the truth" is invariably the preface to bad news: "Frankly, that hat makes you look older." I've yet to hear said, "To tell you the truth, you look perfectly beautiful." I'd be as gentle of others' sensibilities, as polite to my children and children-in-law, as I try to be to people outside the family. I've been appalled by the rudeness of relatives to each other ever since the time I had dinner with a girl's family and listened to an exchange of insults across the table that would have set them all up for a good punch in the mouth anywhere outside the sanctuary of the home. Home is no sanctuary for rudeness. I thought so then, think so now. Of course, the Mount Everest of boorishness is rudeness in front of outsiders, for it presents them with horrendous choices: should they smile, change the subject, or pretend they didn't hear? Surely home is where you can find a sanctuary from snipers' bullets, flying glass, and hidden mines in the war of competition outside? In theory, there is no logical reason to be rude to anybody; above all, where is the logic in being polite to a waiter and rude to your loved ones?

If, in a family discussion, I should be pushed for advice, I'll see that it takes the form of a suggestion easily identified by a phrase like "You might try this . . ." rather than a rigid dictum. The components that make up my children's problems are different from mine when I was young. Theirs is a different battlefield, theirs a different enemy. As an old veteran, I can only suggest how I won my victories. I wouldn't be afraid to let them know how I lost my battles. My defeats could serve to reassure them that they can lose a battle and win the war. After all, I must have managed somehow to pick myself up, brush off the mud, and fight again. I'm still here, aren't I?

Sometimes a reminiscence can light a candle. One daughter has reported that an incident I told her about long ago has helped her through many tense moments in her business life. I was miserable in a new job as assistant to a buyer who was a four-hundred-carat egomaniac, who demeaned me with snapped commands in front of other people, as well as when we were alone, that no self-respecting galley slave could endure. I thought I was stuck with only two alternatives: to become her fawning sycophant, or quit and become her ex-assistant, until my father suggested a third: try out the nonresistance of Mahatma Gandhi. It worked so well that she ended up recommending me for a top buyer's job.

When I do use an incident in my past as a solution for a problem in my children's present, I won't make allusions to people unless I identify them to the son- or daughter-in-law. I'll never presume that they know those whom my children or I know from our shared past.

If a family situation should arise that could better be resolved by my son's or daughter's advice alone, or is a problem that would serve only to bore or harass his wife or her husband, I'll arrange for a lunch with the child whose opinion I seek. Or if I feel a spot of reminiscing coming on, suggest an impulsive meeting with either one. I won't disrupt any household with daily interminable telephone calls. I won't be a Cassandra, with a ghoul's appetite for spreading news of disasters.

I'll keep my mouth shut tight when they whine, complain, or moan against the slings and arrows of their current outrageous fortune. I'll keep an understanding nod handy, but not too much tea and sympathy, for sympathy can dilute their supply of courage. I'll never suggest as an out to a grueling situation that they come home to Mother. Not on the heartless principle that "you've made your bed, you can lie in it." I'll always provide a sanctuary, but on a strictly temporary basis. I'll gladly offer my home for their early convalescence, but I would only delay their recovery if I invited them back into the womb. For my children won't be children anymore when they are married. If their world does go to pieces they have got to be their own architects of a new one.

I'll never drag up their defeats but will remind them of their victories. I'll praise extravagantly every manifestation of courage and generosity. I'll follow Picasso's words: "I give you a little sympathy—you give me back a bit of affection. This is how we both remain alive—a warm current is established that carries us through."

I'll never invade their privacy. I shall be honored by their confidences and will keep their secrets from other members of the family if requested, but never dig with leading questions into their finances, their friends, their bed life.

I shall make no demands upon their time. Never ask them

to do boring errands for me, so long as I'm still on my feet, never, if I'm out of town, write them to run down to Mott Street and send me a pound of the thousand-year-old pickled dragon's teeth that I relish.

I will never make a visit to me a chore they must face. I won't be responsible for the groan "This is the Sunday we have to go to your mother's." Setting a specific day for visits transforms what could be a happy reunion into an appointment with the dentist.

If I'm invited to their place, I'll remember that I am a guest in another woman's house. (I'll never drop in uninvited, of course.) As a guest, I'll follow their ground rules. I'll conform to their schedule of meals and bedtime. I won't outsit my hosts. I'll leave them free time to be by themselves by retiring to my room with the book I remembered to bring, and with my reading glasses that I will remember where I put. (I'll remember to clean my glasses often, not wait for an offspring to remind me to wash them when I complain, "I must need new glasses. I can't see anything anymore.") If a discussion about money should turn into an eyeball-to-eyeball contest between husband and wife, I'll remember I've got a phone call to make and retreat from the battlefield.

The three most dangerous terrains for a visiting mother or mother-in-law are the kitchen, the bathroom, and the viewing space in front of the TV. In the kitchen, safety lies in eating what you're offered, and in bringing some food with you, if you are a between-meal nibbler. In drinking what you are offered, not asking plaintively, "Do you think I could possibly have a Pink Lady?" One glass of the sherry they bought just for you won't kill you even if you hate it.

You'll offer to help with the cooking but not be hurt if your offer is refused. And you'll offer to do the dishes afterward and not be surprised if you're taken at your word.

You'll get in and out of the bathroom fast, especially in the morning, when the rest of the family is rushing to get to work or school. You'll keep your beauty routines and your long soaks in the tub for when the house is empty.

At TV time, you'll watch their favorite programs, not yours. If you're hooked on *Bonanza*, you can miss it for one week: things don't change that fast at the Ponderosa; the boys will all be there, up to their old tricks, next week when you're back in your own little home. You'll always, unless an emergency dictates otherwise, remember the homily: "Fish and guests in three days are stale." The solution guaranteed to please everyone concerned is to stay at a nearby hotel for the duration of your visit, if you can possibly swing it financially. If you can't, keep your visit down to the minimum.

If you are a guest when other guests are expected for a posh dinner, you can eat and run to your bedroom or plead a convenient attack of the vapors and take a tray to your room if you feel your presence might dampen the fun.

You will be shocked by nothing that your children or their guests say. Your acceptance of the new mores does not commit you to approval or disapproval of them. A friend gave me a shining example when she got a telephone call from her grandson telling her he had just been married. When she asked him if he and his bride were planning a honeymoon, his answer was, "Grandma, we've already had three." Her graceful reply was, "Autres temps, autres moeurs."

When you invite your children to your house, you'll often find that you and they will enjoy the visit more if you invite them one couple at a time. Every person in a family can love every other member, but they still may not blend together successfully as a group.

When your family comes to visit you, you'll suspend your own ground rules. You're old enough to accept changes in your routine for a few hours. You'll certainly not try to change their habits or their ways of raising their children. You'll remember what they like to eat and drink and have plenty of both on hand. If they are in the early stages of trying to make ends meet, you'll spoil them with steaks and with fruit that's out of season, even if you have to live on Kraft's Macaroni Dinners for the week after. If they bring with them the added bounty of their children, have a drawerful of small presents you've been collecting. And before any young children arrive, put out of reach the treasures you cherish, so that there will be no tears when a child is told, "You broke Grandma's favorite vase."

In their house or yours, you'll give your children the joy of spoiling you. You won't bridle at the implication that you are ready for the glue factory when they ask you if you are in a draft or when they offer to thread your needle. You won't protest when a grandchild is asked to get up and give the comfortable seat to Grandma. Or to Step-Grandma, a role not unique in this century of multiple marriages. Being a stepmother was a very happy experience for me, because I was fortunate enough to acquire a dear boy as a stepson. And because my guardian angel gave me the wisdom to try to be his friend, not to attempt to compete as a mother, with his real mother.

Circumstances prevent my being a step-grandmother to his children, which is my loss, for to be any kind of grandmother is to be a very happy woman. It's the most relaxed role of all the many parts a woman plays in her life. She doesn't have the responsibility of the grandchild, so that he or she comes under the heading of pure velvet. She is not responsible for the child's manners, except to serve as an exemplary illustration to follow. She would interrupt a bishop's sermon before a child's story. She has the leisure to listen. She has the time to take a grandson to lunch, to ask him to order and play the host. She has it in her power to make every visit a party, if she is a wise grandmother, who is aware of how much the young and old have in common. They share a sense of wonder. To a child his first ride on a ferryboat is a new and astonishing experience. To a grandmother who hasn't taken the time from a crowded life to go aboard, it's a delightful event. Neither is concerned with power or position, money or the future. To children, tomorrow is a million years away. Today is the only reality. Instinct has given them that wisdom. Long years of living have revealed it to their grandmothers.

Freed of the necessity to instruct or guide, a grandmother can laugh with her grandchildren at all the absurdities they both see and hear together. (She will never laugh at her grandchildren's mistakes; ridicule for the young can be as lethal as carbon monoxide.) Together they can scorn the false and the phony. Children have a finely-tuned antenna for the phony; the old have learned by experience to detect it.

They both believe in the invisible. The young accept the existence of mythical creatures that they can't see; the old, a God, or the good in man that they can't behold. The young

have forgotten yesterday. The old remember it as history
and like to return to it in stories of the old days. Small children relish these stories so long as they are histories, not
moral tracts. To them, you are a visitor from another planet.
You can answer their question, "What was it like there?"

Grandmothers and grandchildren often have equal attention spans. At least mine is as short as my grandchildren's. I
grow impatient quickly with their jokes repeated endlessly
because I laughed at their first telling. I want to go take a
nap when they want to play the seventeenth game of Fish.
For us both to enjoy each other's company, I have to take
them in small gulps.

The only restraint I have around them is occasioned by
my fear that a throwaway line of mine will stick like a burr
in their minds for the rest of their lives. Children themselves
are not our only immortality. We live on in the remarks we
make around them. Now part of a third generation is "If
you can't say something nice, don't say anything at all," a
line that I stole from Bambi to give to a daughter twenty-
five years ago and that I heard a granddaughter say yesterday.

My list of guidelines for being a good mother-in-law
turned out to be a long one. And one not easy to follow. But
who has ever contended that it is easy to get along with people? Especially with people who fill the air with emotional
vibrations of earlier memories and rivalries in the most com-
plex of all interlocking relationships—the family?

It should be easy for me. Of course all my children and
grandchildren are remarkable, but I've also been shot with

luck in my in-laws. My son chose a girl who is ridiculously easy to love. A daughter found a man who is impossible not to love. And still I slip up. Only yesterday I heard myself saying to my dear son-in-law about his wife, "Of course I know what she'd like to have better than you do. You've only known her for three years. I've known her all her life." I should have been ashamed. I was.

XII

There's Always Money
for the Movies

❧❦❧

Money is the most personal of all topics. If you doubt it, ask someone how much money she's making. In these franker times, she will tell you everything you ever wanted to know about her sex life. But the amount of her paycheck? Never. The reason is obvious. Success is measured by how much money we have. So if you're not drawing down big money or on your way to making it, you are a failure. In this materialistic age, a poor man or woman is rated one short rung below a murderer.

Certainly in marriage money shares equal billing with sex. Money, a top-drawer lawyer told me, is responsible for more divorces than sex, or rather, the way a man and wife *feel* about money. Too often, it is a subject that is never broached before the wedding. It isn't until after the honeymoon that the bride and groom discover that they belong to two diametrically opposed schools, so far apart as to make any generation gap look like a skip and a jump.

One school regards money as something to be spent. At an amusement park they head straight for the roller coasters and find exhilarating fun in the violent ups and downs of the ride. The other school looks around for the children's merry-go-round. There, firmly clasping the brass pole as they sit on the miniature horses, they find safety. One of the few pieces of advice I permitted myself to offer my children without invitation was to suggest that when they fell in love and planned to make it official, they bring the question of money right out in the open between them.

I'm an old alumna of the roller-coaster school, which probably explains why I now have no money. I grew up in a time when it wasn't considered "nice" to talk about money. To this day I haven't the least idea how much money my father had. When I asked him, "Are we rich or poor?" he told me, "Neither. We are smack in the middle." It was an answer that gave a child no measuring stick. So that when Father told me I couldn't go on a pleasure trip, it never occurred to me that he didn't have the money for my train tickets. I thought I'd picked a bad day to ask him.

My ignorance was hard on a young husband. I met him, coming home one night from his poorly paid job, at the door of our semidetached studio with the news that the man wouldn't bring any coal because we hadn't paid for the previous delivery. "Okay," he said, "we'll just have to freeze until payday." "No, we won't," I told him. "You can write him a check." When he answered, "I can't. There isn't any money in the bank," I turned as white as the sheet in a Duz commercial because I thought there was always *some* money in the bank.

Many years of having a balance of $1.39 in my checking account the day before payday have taught me the absurdity of that vacuous reaction. But I still have no reverence for money. I was around during the Depression. I saw too many men who had been provident, who had made safe investments to provide for that rainy day, lose everything and become desperate. It conditioned me to relish Gene Fowler's description: "Money is something to throw off the back of trains." I've always spent the money I earned as fast as I could run to the bank to cash the check.

I've been amazed at rich people's attitude toward money. The memory of the bewildered look I caught in a young boy's eyes keeps it greening. His father had monopolized the conversation at a dinner party in the country with his whines about the high tuition at his son's school. "I can't pay it," he whimpered hysterically. "I don't have that kind of money. I don't have *any* money." As he got up from the table, he turned to me. "Come on out and see my prize bull that was just shipped up from Virginia. He's a beauty. And at $5,000, he's a bargain." My censor must have been asleep when I answered, "But I thought you didn't have any money," for he gave me a patronizing stare before he answered, "This is different. He is an investment." That was when I caught the bewildered look in his son's eyes.

The bull represented to his father an investment in safety. And the rich want above all else to be safe, because most of them are frightened people. They feel that money is their only armor; without it they would be naked before their enemies. That generality may have its roots in jealousy, of course. Perhaps you have it easier, but *my* hardest chore is being honest with myself. Even so, I think I'm honest in my belief that only one's courage is responsible for one's safety. And every year demands more courage—courage to match the exhortation of an old warrior found in an early English poem, "Mind must be firmer, heart the more fierce, courage the greater, as your strength diminishes." It is your courage that supplies the adrenalin to face the ups and the downs and, with the addition of ingenuity and imagination, come up with enough money to handle both. That father with the $5,000 bull would think such a philosophy mad if I had told him, but I believe, with Gorki, that the madness of the brave is the wisdom of life.

The sixties' call for bravery is loud and clear. You may be one of the provident who has a goodly supply of stocks and bonds or who has a husband with a pension. The two of you may well have chosen the blueprint for your future long ago, have picked the place where you plan to live, the house you are going to live in. You are so affectionately familiar with its landscape that you even know the shape of the leaves on the tree before its door. If you're not married, you may still have a pension coming to you that will be the key to your dream cottage, or if a widow, enough insurance to serve the same purpose.

If upon retirement you can anticipate no pension or no insurance, the withdrawals from your courage bank are heavier. The right of choice is still yours, though the selection has diminished.

You would be wise, before you make any financial move, to seek the advice of a banker or lawyer, not an acquaintance. Widows are still losing their mites by following the advice of "that nice young man, who's the nephew of my oldest friend." A respectable balance in the bank presents two choices. You can use it to pay for your present bed and board while you look for a postretirement job, or you can blow it all on a down payment on a cottage if, like Padraic Colum's Old Woman of the Roads, you've always longed to have a little house, a house of your own. You, like her,

> . . . could be quiet there at night
> Beside the fire and by myself,
> Sure of a bed and loth to leave
> The ticking clock and the shining delph!

You could live there, out of the wind's and the rain's way. That is, if you could beg or borrow enough to supplement your social security pension.

If I had any juices left over from job-hunting, I would use them to organize a sixties' march to Washington to bring to the President's attention the paradox in our present Social Security setup. Our scientists are discovering more and more ways to prolong life. (In 1970, over 20 million Americans were sixty-five and over.) But many of our businessmen are retiring older workers faster and faster. There is a fairly well substantiated rumor that the retirement age of sixty, mandatory in many firms, will be lowered to fifty-five in a few years. How are older people supposed to fill the added years science is giving them? Not by working. Even if at their unpopular age they find a job, they can only earn a miniscule sum. Any more reasonable amount threatens their old-age pension. The government makes one generous concession: after seventy-two, it allows them to earn as much as they like. How much can people earn at seventy-two? And what do they live on in the interim between their retirement and their seventy-second birthday?

Stipulated, as the federal lawyers would say, the old-age pension was not planned to provide an entire income, but to supplement what money older people had. But the hard truth is that many retired people have no income to supplement. Retirement has become a national as well as a personal crisis.

Even if there are grown children to help, there is the older people's pride to consider, as well as their loving compassion for their children who are facing the responsibilities of raising and educating their own children. With higher prices and lower salaries, parents are reluctant to add their financial burdens to those of their children. They are equally reluctant to move in with them. Aside from the strain that mixing generations brings, there isn't room for them. When living in a house was the norm and an apartment the exception, there was an extra room where a grandmother could live, among her own lares and penates. On call to baby-sit, but her own woman in her own room. To find an apartment or a house with one separate bedroom for the children is cause for rejoicing today. And for many of us the cutoff of our income isn't the only problem. For those of us who have found joy in our jobs, a life without work stretches out ahead, an endless, arid desert. It is a tragic paradox.

Whatever financial setup you face in your sixties, you

would be wise to realize some changes are necessary in your attitude about money. One of the most popular sports is to criticize the way other people spend their money. Mark Twain said, "Nothing so needs reforming as other people's habits." One person's extravagance is another's necessity. To redefine mine, I had to figure out the minimum amount I would need to pay for the three demands on my pocketbook. I needed money for Essentials. Under that heading I originally put rent, food, taxis. I needed money for Crises. Sickness, loans to friends in grave trouble, trips essential to business or family, upkeep or replacement of household equipment or of clothes. Under the third heading, Carnival Money, went dinner parties, long-distance calls, presents to others and to myself, movies and plays, books and flowers.

I hope there will be enough Carnival Money for me to give my children presents at unexpected times. I'll send them on the conventional occasions, and I'll send them something that I've found out they want. But I'll surprise them too with a pretty, even a silly bit of nonsense for no reason at all. Or with a spot of money. To open a note and find five dollars is as great as finding forgotten change in an old pocketbook.

If I choose something for them, I will have established the principle early on that they will face no tiresome hurt feelings from me if they exchange it. Whatever I give them will be something extravagant they can't afford themselves: bath salts, a bunch of daisies, a bottle of perfume, a wild pair of boots, a beautiful book on English gardens or old cars. Money's the best present of all—and money with no strings attached (unless a loan has been requested—that's a different kettle of fish). I'll never say, "This is to get a new rug for your hallway—the one you've got down now is a disgrace." Money *is* power. I won't use it to bully. I'll let money be a pleasure, to receive, to spend. That's grace. And I'll accept their thanks with grace. I won't say, "Oh, that old thing" or "I wish I could have given you a better one." And I'll never, when they say, "I'm crazy about it," answer, "You'd better be. It cost enough." Never will I quote the price of the present I give them.

I'll accept their presents, too, with grace, never questioning their extravagance, never saying, "Oh, you shouldn't have." I'll be crazy about whatever they choose. I'll help them out by keeping available a running list of what I'd like to have, with nothing too expensive on it, like a yacht, or a Mercedes Benz, to show them if they should ask what I would like for Christmas.

I used up a tablet of paper before I reached the final divisions of my money lists. By that time I had moved taxis from the Essential list to the one headed Crises. I had moved books and flowers from Carnival to Essential. I am, as a granddaughter introduced me to a friend, a booker. I've lived a literary life, with characters from novels for friends, with lines of poetry for battle cries. Flowers also moved to the Essential list, for to watch a hyacinth bursting into blue on my table is to renew my faith in miracles.

I have been indescribably fortunate. I have never missed a meal, never had to worry about where the next one was coming from. So I have never been poor, or as we are supposed to say now, disadvantaged. But I've been strapped enough to worry about where I'd find the next month's rent. In those times, I remembered Mama, in that TV series you doubtless recall, too, with affection. In family crises

Mama would say, "We'll have to go to the bank." It wasn't until the last segment of the series that you were let in on the secret that Mama's Bank Account was a dish where she put all the loose change she had managed to save. I borrowed Mama's idea. I was exhilarated to find that by demoting what I had considered Essentials to the status of Extravagance, I had saved enough in my dish to bring home a hyacinth to feed my soul.

My hard times educated me in other ways. They taught me that there was no loss of self-respect in asking doctors, lawyers, and dentists if they had a sliding scale for their fees. (I found out most of them do.) They taught me there's nothing wrong with bargain-hunting, but it's wrong to bore other people with your triumphs. I learned that even when it's necessary to cut corners, there's no need to be obvious about it, like writing letters on old scraps of paper. It's better to spend $2.00 on a box of stationery and go without meat for a couple of days, than to demonstrate to your correspondents that you have become a professional poor little old lady. I learned too that if I shared my apartment or the tab for a trip with a friend, I'd see to it that a businesslike, written-down budget would be agreed upon before the beginning of either experience. If I should ever have to live with any of my family or take financial help from them, I'll remember that lesson.

Depending on where you're standing, I've been (mildly) rich. I've been (mildly) poor. I have found that rich *is* better. I think money is the prettiest green thing in the world that isn't growing. It can bring freedoms, the freedom to choose where you live, what kind of house you live in, what kind of view you see when you look out the window. It can give you freedom from some of the horrors of poverty—the overcrowding, the vermin, the noise, the scary neighborhood, the insistent smell of poverty. Money gives you the freedom to be independent. Best of all, it gives you the freedom to be useful to other people. That is when money changes from pretty to beautiful.

But if my eventual blueprint is colored poor, I will still have a choice: I can be a defeated poor relative, or a proud old lady. I hope I'll find the courage to choose the proud old lady, who will throw her last nickel off the back of a train.

XIII

Whistling in the Dark

Few people greet the arrival of old age with a brass band. It's not old age we dread. It is the villains who travel with him: poverty and sickness, loneliness and death. With daring and imagination we can conquer the first three or, by refusing to let them intimidate us, can cut them down to size. Death is a tougher enemy. He is no enemy to those with a faith that promises a future life. I felt a twinge of envy when I once read: "The people in Russia hold God in their hearts like a man carrying a lantern under his coat on a stormy night." But the only prayer I know by heart is one written by Robert Louis Stevenson, which is more like a bugle calling me to try to be a decent woman, than a prayer: "To be honest, to be kind—to earn a little and spend a little

less, to make upon the whole a family happier for his presence, to renounce when that shall be necessary and not to be
embittered, to keep a few friends, but these without capitu-
lation—above all, on the same grim condition, to keep
friends with himself—here is a task for all that a man has of
fortitude and delicacy."

I envy those of strong faith but cannot emulate them. I'll
not "go gentle into that good night." I shall "rage, rage."
And I will defy Death's attempts to panic me. Panic is one
of his most vicious weapons. He'll try to beat me to a pulp
with fears before he lands his knockout punch.

A woman's desolation over the death of a beloved husband is often heightened by her panic over the future.
There is not much a friend can do to dispel her panics except to offer the comfort of her company. Nobody should be
alone to face the shock of a surprise attack. You will be valuable to her because you are *there*. You will leave at home all
the maxims that you may have tried as incantations to scare
away your own panics, like "This, too, shall pass" and
"Nothing is so much to be feared as fear" and "Present fears
are less than horrible imaginings." You won't bring along
practical suggestions about jobs or money; those can come
later, when she's convalescing from fear. (There's nothing
to stop your writing her a check, if you can. Immediate
money is a quick palliative to terror.) You won't give her
fast clips on the jaw with "Come on, stop feeling sorry for
yourself," or "Snap out of it," or "You think you've got
troubles?"

The only luggage you bring with you is your love. You
withhold your judgment, your criticism, and your advice;
you make another pot of coffee and you listen.

The only justification for advice is when your friend shows signs that she is going to embark immediately on a drastic change in her life pattern, for hasty decisions impelled by panic can be disastrous. In the loneliness of her husband's sudden death, a friend of mine abruptly quit an exhilarating job, sold her pleasant house, and moved to Italy. All she found there was an alien loneliness. When she came back to New York, she faced two ugly realities: the paucity of exhilarating jobs and of decent places to live.

It's usually a mistake to make any move in any direction until the panics have subsided and you can think again. And make no mistake: you can't think when the panics take over. They make you an invalid by atrophying your sixth sense, the one most necessary for your survival: your sense of humor, which is your personal sense of proportion. You need a visiting nurse. Don't be ashamed to admit it. Call for help. It's not pride, but vanity that stops you from asking. You may want your friends and family to think of you as a bigger-than-life heroine. They will love you no less if they see you when you are a heroine momentarily reduced to life size. Don't be selfish. Give your family and friends the joy of being needed by you.

Sometimes you do find a solution when you hit bottom. An artist with seven children told me he had been awakened many nights with the fearful thought, "What will happen to them if I don't sell a picture? If there's no money in the house?" One morning what he feared most occurred. The milkman refused to leave the seven bottles of milk until his bill was paid. There was no money in the house. My friend walked four miles to the local office of the P.W.A. and bulldozed his way to a loan and a commission for a mural. "I've never been afraid again," he told me. "The worst happened and we survived it." But with no children as an incentive, or no talent to barter with, some of us can find no answer when we hit the bottom of the barrel.

Until all the panics are subdued, it is better and safer to stay in familiar surroundings, with familiar faces. The kind hearts and gentle people of your hometown can't cure sorrows or panics, but they can make them easier to endure.

It's wise, if a change of scene continues to seem like a good idea, to arrange for a trial run of the new life before you break up the old. If a foreign country beckons, go there as a tourist, try it out for a short spell before you ship over your furniture. Consider your prejudices. If you don't like heat, you're not going to like the hot days in Jamaica any more than you do at home in Missouri. If primitive art has never appealed to you, you won't like it any better when you see it in Mexico. If you've always preferred the ocean to the desert, you will leave the Big Sky to John Wayne.

If you've always been a city woman who dreams every spring of a lilac bush blooming by a doorway, go to the country for a couple of months before you break your lease. Go in the winter. If you are of a contemplative bent, you may find joy in the silence and solitude of a country life. But if you are alive only when, as E. M. Forster says, "you connect" with other people, you will feel you have chosen loneliness as your companion. Don't burn your bridges until you have tried out your dream, or you may find yourself sitting in its ruins.

If sharing a house or an apartment with an old friend bobs up as a pleasing vision, it is wise to try a few months of communal living first. Living with a husband doesn't prepare you for living in the same house with a woman friend. You and your husband had shared enough things together to build up an acceptance of each other's idiosyncrasies. There is no such backlog of tolerance to ease the sometimes abrasive meshing of two women's habits. After all, the Chinese knew what they were up to when they chose two women under the same roof as their symbol for trouble. If you have lived by yourself for any length of time, you will find it irritating to have to put the top back on the toothpaste again.

Nevertheless, living with a peer holds out a comforting and comfortable promise. You share the same points of reference. You don't have to identify a Doreen or a Bramley. You can swap nostalgias. You share the same likes and dislikes, which are even more satisfying (you both loved *The Green Hat*, both hated *If Winter Comes*). You must share a goodly sum of them or you wouldn't be friends. And you admire each other. We do, as Wordsworth noted, "live by admiration, hope, and love." It would be an untenable existence to live in the same house with a woman who was patently only putting up with you because you were paying half the rent.

It's a grim thought but one that must be said: it's a mistake to move to a town or country that holds no charms for you only in order to be near a friend. Because death may come gunning for your friend before you, and you would be left alone, in an unhappy climate.

But then death is not compassionate. I hate death. I think the more you enjoy life, the more you hate death. I've never understood how anyone could commit suicide. Messy and horrible as life can become, I still don't want to miss a moment of it. Suicide is very bad manners, anyway. It causes trouble and guilt for those left behind. It probably isn't character that puts me on the side of life, but good health that gives me the resilience to bounce back after a knockdown. But even when I can no longer be a performer, being an interested spectator will still be preferable to not being there at all.

I should be grateful to death. He once did me a favor. We had a brief encounter, but it was long enough for me to learn to substitute "when I die" for "if I die." The acceptance that death was inevitable gave the next twenty-four hours a vast importance. It taught me to realize that if my time was limited I couldn't waste a moment of it. I wouldn't wait for explicit events to occur before I enjoyed today— put off my pleasure in living until my son got a "good" job or until my daughter married a "nice" boy. I wouldn't wait until another day to tell someone that I love them, or better still, to show them that I love them. If I recognize that today could be the only day I have, I'm not going to use up any of its precious moments criticizing or condemning. I want to be sure to remind someone how pretty she is, or how kind he is. All of us, when our parents die, wish we had told them how important they were to us, had told our father what an example of gentleness he gave us, or told our mother what a high standard of wit she set for her family.

I'm not going to sit around waiting for death, immobilized by fear. Not if I can help it. Everyone has to find her own weapon to fight fear. Mine is being a ham. I'm going to act brave, am going to act as if I were enjoying every minute I've got. I'll convince my children that death is not the enemy, but the fear of death. And maybe I'll be good enough to convince myself.

If I had a choice, I'd like to go out the way nature has arranged it for trees in the fall. They go out in a blaze of color, in defiant shouts of red and yellow before their leaves turn brown and fall off the trees. "Live," said Death to Virgil, "for I am coming." When Death comes for me, I hope I'll be so busy working and laughing, I won't hear his knock. He'll have to break down the door to get in.

XIV

Time on Your Hands

Stay beautiful
but dont stay down underground too long
Dont turn into a mole
or a worm
or a root
or a stone

Come on out into the sunlight
Breathe in trees
Knock out mountains
Commune with snakes
& be the very hero of birds

Dont forget to poke your head up
& blink
think
Walk all around
Swim upstream

Dont forget to fly*

Leisure, in the sixties, is a two-time thing. It can be a prison, with fears as jailers, or it can be a 747 jet that can fly you to enjoyment. How you use your leisure will determine whether it is a gift or a catastrophe. "I'm keeping Fielding to enjoy in my seventies," a white-haired woman was heard to say in a bookstore. I'm not going to wait until my seventies to enjoy my favorite hobby, which is traveling. I can start today. I don't need to pack a suitcase, leave a note for the milkman, take a taxi to the airport. All my trip requires is a comfortable chair, a cup of coffee, imagination, and I'm off. Once aboard the Time Unlimited Express, I can go where I please. I am a traveler in time.

I can travel backward in time, can visit any country at any time in its history. If I choose to visit England, I can also choose which of her queens I'd like to be. I'd have a vigorous and lusty life if I picked Elizabeth, the first Elizabeth. It would be heady stuff to have Shakespeare write a play for me and to send ships over unknown horizons on uncharted seas. But there would be the cruelties and violence of the Elizabethan age to face. And the smells around the castles must have been horrendous.

I might choose Victoria when she was the young queen,

* "For Poets," by Al Young.

not when she grew old and cantankerous and silly about John Brown. But even young, I'd be stuck with Albert, who was a worthy bore, and that's the worst kind. It would be delectable to be the reigning beauty of an era, like Queen Alexandra, but then I'd have Edward VII on my hands. He charmed all those ladies with the hourglass figures, during all those long weekends in the stately homes of England, but I have a hunch that when he was alone with his own family, he belched out loud.

I can hold up the train long enough for a spending spree, because, next to me, Jackie Onassis is a penny-pincher. First, I will set up the usual billion-dollar trust funds for my children and their children and for my son-in-law and my daughter-in-law. Everybody will have the freedom of choice that money can bring, and the freedom to spend it as he or she wishes. I'm not giving anybody money to use as a club to bully anyone else. Then I shall become a big investor in real estate. I'll buy a castle in Killarney, a houseboat on the Seine, a saltbox on Nantucket, a flat in Belgrave Square, a brownstone on East Eighty-second Street, and a lighthouse in Antigua. I'll throw in a couple who will go on ahead to air the rooms and turn down the beds. I'll make do at the local Ritz until they send back my private plane to pick me up.

While I'm waiting I can roller-skate up Fifth Avenue. Without my billions, the cop would put me down as a crazy old woman and call for the wagon to take me to the booby hatch. With my billions, he will identify me as that eccentric old Mrs. Serendipity, and he'll clear a path through the traffic for me.

Or I can pass the time planning the perfect dinner party. The men that I invite may not like it that I'll be the only woman, but it's my dream party, so they'll have to lump it. The only problem the party presents is who to put in the seat of honor. How can I choose, when the guests will be Yves Montand, Jonathan Miller, Bill Cosby, Richard Burton, Stuart Symington, Paul Newman, Peter De Vries, Dick Cavett, Robert Morley, Duke Ellington, John Cheever, Pablo Picasso, Orson Welles, Peter Ustinov, E. B. White, Federico Fellini, and the beautiful young man I saw on the subway yesterday morning? Three men would be the chief contenders for the place at my right: Orson Welles, Paul Newman, and Peter Ustinov. Orson Welles is one of the three not only because he is this century's most brilliant maverick, but because he said the qualities he most admired in a human being were courage and good manners. It isn't Paul Newman's astonishingly blue eyes that put him in the running, but two of the answers he gave in a TV interview. When David Frost asked him what kept him going, he answered, "Terror." And when asked what plans he had for his future, Paul Newman's answer was "I hope to get through it with some grace and some style." I think Peter Ustinov will be the winner because he finds life a stylish joke. I wouldn't want to miss the chance of laughing at it with him.

I don't need trains or planes or billions to imagine experiences that I've never had. I can enjoy them, freed from the necessity of energy, equipment, or skill. I can ride a cresting wave on Waikiki Beach without a surfboard, climb Mont Blanc without a pick and rope. Without moving a finger, with leisure and a little imagination, I can go around the world in eighty seconds. It's the most entertaining game of solitaire ever invented.

There are other games to play. You can become a collector, perhaps not of coins from Samarkand, but of curious words. You can find delight in tracing the origin of phrases you've used all your life. "What in Sam Hill" heads my word list. Who was Sam? Where was his hill? Or you can explore, if not resolve, the mysteries of the English language. If you can say "It's raining," why not "It's sunning"? You can explore a new language, which will lead you to explore the literature of another country.

You can reread the books you loved when you read them years ago, try again the books whose charms eluded you on the first time around.

You can be, if you watch TV, a cliché collector. "Let me look at you," will surely be on your list, and "He's a real human being," which always brings up the unspoken question, "What else could he be? A real saber-toothed tiger?"

If you have already discovered the pleasures of a hobby, you can give more of your time to its cultivation. If you like flowers—and there is a silly sentence if you're collecting Sillies, for did you ever hear of anybody who *hated* flowers?—but if flowers are on your list of Necessary Things, you will now have time to go to Charleston when the azaleas are in bloom. If you wish to find them in your own backyard, you can sign up for a course in gardening. If your passion is roses, you have the leisure to trace their genealogy. The search will take you so far back in time that you may find yourself the author of *The History of the Rose* before you know it.

You can turn a hobby into a book, as English author

Peter Bull did with his *Teddy Bear Book*. *Time* reported "that when he asked Alice Roosevelt Longworth, after whose father, President Teddy Roosevelt, the cuddly stuffed animal was named, would she mind if he brought along to tea a couple of bears? she would indeed, Bull was informed. 'I may be an old crone,' grumped Princess Alice, 'but I'm not driveling enough to have tea with a Teddy bear.' (Quelle Grande Dame!)" Mr. Bull's book was rather arch, but he obviously enjoyed writing it and it sold. Now you will have the leisure to write the book you always said you were going to write when you had time. But don't be disappointed if you can't sell it to a publisher. Memories don't always make interesting memoirs. And the story you told your grandchild that held her glued to her seat may not appeal to juvenile editors, as a surefire fascinator for other children—understandable if you remember that children will listen to you read the telephone book to them, they are so delighted to have *your* complete attention. But, published or not, you will have the pleasure of creation when you write it.

The adult education courses available in cities, or available by mail if you live in a small town, are as varied as your fancies. These courses will increase your knowledge of subjects that have always interested you or open doors to worlds you never knew existed. Take time to choose before signing up. First my father and then I have paid enough tuition to art galleries for courses in learning to paint to buy an original Renoir for the Metropolitan Museum of Art. I'd go to a couple of sessions and then fade away. It took fifty years to teach me that in art I was meant to be the passenger on the train, not the motorman. As a passenger I can find real joy in a trip to a museum or a gallery.

In sports I, who was never good at any of them, can take delight in being a spectator. You don't have to play tennis to be awed by the precise grace of tennis champions. You can be scared to death of horses but find the patterns of their ordered paces in horse shows beautiful to behold.

You will have time to revive an old delight—the art of letter writing. You can light up an author's day by a note thanking him for the book that brought you pleasure, or a child's by complimenting him on an achievement; or you can let a president of a country or a company know what an articulate curmudgeon thinks of his stupid antics. You can, through a course or on your own, polish back to a high burnish your skill at backgammon or chess, bridge or Russian bank. You will also brighten the time with your grandchildren, for by sharing your revived enthusiasm and knowledge of games with them, you will give them the answer to their stock question, "What can I do now?"

Your leisure can send you on voyages of discovery into new countries of the mind. Your curiosity may prompt a safari into the land of witchcraft and magic. By studying science, you can explore the mysteries of the land and sea and air, by studying philosophy, the mysteries of the human soul.

You have the time to explore new countries of the spirit. Music was an alien land for me. I have a tin ear, and I don't understand music. People who go to concerts and operas usually talk in such solemn tones about music—I have always been suspicious of anything you can't laugh about. But at sixty, I was given a hi-fi and a record by the Swingle Singers of Bach and went wild with joy when I discovered that Bach was joy. When I met up with Isaac Stern's recordings of Bach there was no stopping me: I now possess more Bach than bath towels.

If your social conscience is still greening, you will have the time to work for the election of a man you believe in, or to defeat a candidate you distrust. If your compassion still glows, you will find a world filled with people who are desperately in need of its warmth. Jobs for volunteers are waiting everywhere: in hospitals, clinics, libraries, drug centers, and nurseries, in public service offices, at churches and synagogues. You will help more if your heart is pure; if you come really to help rather than to use the occasion as therapy for your boredom or loneliness. *And* if you come prepared to take orders. Many older women who have been pretty autonomous in their offices or their own homes bridle at taking orders, especially from younger women. Thus they are not helpers, but hinderers.

If you can bring a skill along with you, you will enhance your opportunities to help. If you can type—and if you can't, you'd do well to learn—you will double your usefulness to any organization, for typing skill is what separates the professional from the amateur. If you can read well, read to blind patients. If you've ever acted, devise plays for children.

A young actor friend helped children in the disturbed ward of a hospital put on a play that they had coauthored. The children titled the play *Portia Faces Bellevue*. The afternoon it was presented was a Fourth of July day for everybody: for the children who were the actors, for the doctors and nurses who were their audience, and most of all for the young actor. His gift of time and affection was returned to him manyfold. He discovered that Walt Whitman was right when he wrote, "The love is to the lover and comes back most to him."

If you are not locked into fixed ideas of how you ought to spend your time, you will discover all kinds of occupations you never knew existed. You know about baby-sitters, but have you heard about house-sitters? Look in *The New York Times* or in the personal column of the *Saturday Review*. You may find a house-sitter wanted for a lovely Bahamian house in Nassau or a handsome adobe in Santa Fe—the only rent, your promise to keep the place occupied and aired while its owners are away. Or you may hear of a house-sitting job from friends or acquaintances, if you spread the word near and far that you are available. There are historic houses, too, where you can live rent-free, if you are willing to show tourists through three days a week. If you are a cat lover, you can cat-sit for a season in some spiffy house or apartment. If a flower buff, you can be a garden-sitter. It turns into a great big, wonderful, wacky world of choices when you take your train of thought off the tracks and convert it into a plane with the freedom of the skies.

You will find, if you use your leisure to explore new worlds, great pleasure. And you will give pleasure to your young. They will crow with pride, like the little girl I overheard saying, "Grandma's taking a course in carpentry so she can make me a rowboat for Christmas. And she's eighty. Isn't she terrific?"

She was a magician as well as a terrific Grandma. She had transformed the time on her hands into the time of her life.

XV

Off to See the Wizard

The best thing that can happen to you in the sixties is to find yourself broke. Because the worst thing that can happen to you in the sixties is to find yourself with nothing to do when you wake up in the morning. Having nothing to do turns you into a lost woman. You are lost because you are no longer needed. Many women who have loved their husbands find themselves alone in a void when he dies. Other women find themselves trapped there after a divorce, because divorce is a small death. It is the fading of a flower that two people had planted together with high hopes. A retirement can also pinch-hit as a guide to despair, for to feel unneeded is to feel an intimation of dying.

There is only one way out. Go to work! Don't hesitate!

Get a job at once! And if you're broke, you will have no choice.

Unless you are one of the lucky ones, a woman who found the time and the zest to have both a career and a family, so that when your family's need for you has diminished or has been destroyed by death, you can divert the time and zest devoted to them into the stream of your career. It is the woman who has made her family her career who has to face the deepest despair when her husband dies or leaves her or when she finds herself alone in a house once bursting with children who have left to establish worlds of their own.

Her bank account may be rich as a Rockefeller's and her spirit still be poor if she feels useless. Resort towns as well as big cities are crowded with women whose only problem is not how to meet the rent but how to kill time. You can find them in restaurants and doctors' offices, in bars and boutiques. They are easy to spot: they are the well-dressed women with the fear of an empty tomorrow in their eyes.

"Why should I bother to get up?" a woman once cried to me. I wish I could have answered, "Because you have to go to work." If she had asked me instead how she could find a job I could have been more useful to her. I could have given her the road map that a generous friend had given me, in which I found my escape route from hopelessness.

Annie found me looking through the "Help Wanted—Female" columns in *The New York Times*. "Put that paper down," she commanded. "You can't look for a job until you write a résumé." All the jobs I'd ever had had been given to me by friends. I didn't know what a résumé was, so she told me, "It tells what kind of work you've done, where you've done it, when you did it, how much you were paid, why you quit. It's like a business autobiography. It gives your vital statistics, your age and sex and stuff like that. And there's a place on it for your personal, financial, and business references." The last feature panicked me. I could come up with a couple of personal references, but no business ones— I hadn't worked for fifteen years. I'd have to leave the space for financial references blank too, because my credit rating was blank.

Annie wasn't discouraged. "Okay, we'll make a different kind of résumé. We'll make a résumé about you that will tell you who you are. We'll make a list of all the things you don't like and all the things you do like; then you can go gunning for a job that matches up with the Like column."

The résumé turned into a game of truth or consequences, as she invented more and more questions to shoot at me. Rather, she devised more and more choices I had to make. Some were practical, some were philosophical.

> Do you like to get out of the house or stay at home?
> Do you like to live in the country or the city?
> Do you like to spend your leisure time reading or watching TV?
> Do you like to cook or eat out?
> Do you like to make your own clothes or buy them?
> Do you like to shop or avoid it?
> Do you like to write letters or receive them?
> Do you like to save money or spend it?
> Do you find facts and figures fascinating or do they bore you?

Do you like to be alone or with other people?

Do you like to inaugurate a new project or make one work?

Do you like to tell people what to do or have them direct you?

Do you like to take a chance or play it safe?

Do you expect people to be decent or no damned good?

My friend wrote down my answers, then said, "The solution is obvious. You should look for a job in a big city, selling clothes or books." "Well, it's not obvious to me," I said. "How did you arrive at it?" "It was simple. You don't like to live in the country. You have no domestic skills you could develop at home. You wouldn't like any job you could do at home, anyway, because you'd rather get out of the house and be with people. You like the city. You like people. Stores have plenty of people in them. You will like selling books or clothes because both interest you. You'll be good at selling because you like people. Q.E.D. Look for a job in a store in a big city."

"Amazing, my dear Evangeline Adams!" I said.

"That's only the half of it," Annie said smugly. "The answers also indicate that you'll also be willing to start at a very small salary. It won't take you long to ask for a job with more responsibility and authority, and with any luck you'll get it. You may even write a book if you can arrange to have a desk smack in the middle of Grand Central Station. Wait and see if I'm not right."

Amazingly enough, she was. I looked for and found a job in a New York bookstore as a saleswoman, a job that I enjoyed. Ranking high among the reasons why was because there were men there. Women's Lib may drum me out of the regiment for saying it, but I've been man-crazy ever since I fell in love at fourteen with Richard Barthelmess. For me, a life without men in it would be as incomplete a design as yin without yang. Later, luck gave me the chance to become the children's book buyer. I was able to hold onto the position for eight rich and happy years because I was working at a job that I enjoyed. I even wrote a book about it.

Annie's questions and my answers were my magic map. It was fortunate that I kept it, for I was able to lend it to friends when they were confused and bewildered about their futures. Their answers were different, and so were the solutions their answers brought. Only one element stayed constant—my friends have all found enjoyment in jobs where they can work at what they like best to do.

In some instances, their self-summations caused them to consider creating jobs for themselves. If they liked to stay at home and were famous for their beef stew, they could make up an enormous kettle of it and sell it as their specialty— first to friends, then, packed in plastic dishes, to their friendly butcher. They could offer, through an ad in their local paper, a Dial-a-Stew Service. Every town has its quota of lazy women like me who would gladly use the telephone rather than the stove. Or they could offer a loaf of their cracked-wheat bread to the public and find to their pleased surprise that they are suddenly the president of a vast chain of bakeries, as did Margaret Rudkin, the founder of Pepperidge Farm.

If they enjoyed running a house but no longer had one to run, they could apply for a post as a house mother in a boarding school, or as housekeeper for a career woman. Some older women feel that a position as a domestic is demeaning. Not today. Housekeepers and cooks can command high salaries and luxurious living conditions. And if they should find the treatment they received demeaning, all they would have to do is insert an ad in the paper. Then their only problem would be which new offer to accept.

If they liked to sew, they could achieve the status of a pearl without price if they offered, for a nominal fee, to turn up or lower a hem. Or they could start a sewing school in their neighborhood. Or if they were a whiz with the knitting or embroidery needle, a school for knitting or crewel embroidery or gros or petit point. The present is a lucky time for women who have made a craft a hobby, for there is now a resurgence of interest in all crafts—crotcheting, knitting, sewing, paper-folding, lace-making, embroidery.

They could develop the skills to qualify for typing jobs to do at home; if they liked facts, research projects. If they wanted to live in the country and loved flowers, they could go knocking at the door of a nursery for a part time job; if they were silly about dogs, seek out a kennel.

If they were good executives, they could organize special services for other executives. They could run errands for a career woman, buy her Christmas presents for her, take her wig to Kenneth's.

Or they could be the promoters or lobbyists for services that other women have thought of but are not good saleswomen enough to sell by themselves. Or they could collect other women to form a company that offers shopping or other services, by phone or in person.

The necessity for enjoying the job you do grows increasingly important as you grow older. The quality of your zest may be as limitless as when you were a young thing, but its quantity has gone down on the scale. It will be more of a drag to pull off the covers on a dreary February morning. But you'll force yourself to get up, and you'll be happy you did when you get to work if you find pleasure waiting there for you. (Practical note: if you go looking for part-time work, you would do well to volunteer for the earlier shifts. You will also guarantee yourself a grateful welcome from the younger members of the staff.)

Pleasure and work are suspect as a combination to many ears. "It's all very well to have fun in your leisure time" is their contention, "but work is no fun. Work is—well, it's work." Balderdash! is my answer. If work isn't fun, it's not work, it's a numbing, exhausting chore. You'll go through the working hours like a zombie, and you'll be rated N for No-Good Zombie as well. If you make your hobby your job, you will be good at it, because you will enjoy it.

Job possibilities are as varied as the characters of the women who seek them. (There's a valuable paperback available that can suggest jobs you might not have imagined. Its title: *Not Quite Ready to Retire: 351 Jobs and Businesses for Older Workers.* It's written by William David, published by Collier Books.) The women who find the job that gives them cash and contentment are the women who know what they like, what they enjoy. And they have found more than cash and contentment. They have found freedom, freedom from loneliness and from a sense of uselessness.

I've gone back to Annie's list and quizzed myself. The answers form a different road map now that I am sixty-seven than they did when I was fifty-two.

I can find no road on the current map that goes to Alice Roosevelt Longworth's house. I am not sorry I considered her as a woman to emulate. Thinking about her as the character I would like to play added important subtleties to the role I have chosen. I can't be, like her, a Great Lady, but I shall try to be a Life-Enhancer. I shall try to welcome each added year as a promise, not a threat. I shall try to be a "woman amused, serene and whole." I shall try above all to play my role with grace.

I don't believe an ersatz Mrs. Longworth would be happy in the role that I now think will best become my present skills and resources. I want to close down the current performance. I want to take on a totally different part in a play that's yet to be produced. I need the danger of trying to play a different kind of character. Safety makes me lazy.

I don't know what the setting will be, but somewhere a coffee house may soon open its doors. In it will be a huge bulletin board covering the back wall. Printed across it in exuberant big green letters will be another prayer by Robert Louis Stevenson: "Give us grace and strength to forbear and to persevere. Give us courage and gaiety and the quiet mind." Beneath those words older women who have dropped in for coffee will be able to read or tack up notices of jobs available, services offered, and skills to exchange. I hope they will find laughter there too, and friendship. I planned at first to call my coffee house The Phoenix Exchange Post, but that was too obvious.

I will call it The Joyful Woman.

THE END